Food from your
forest garden

Food from your
forest garden

How to harvest, cook and preserve your forest garden produce

MARTIN CRAWFORD and CAROLINE AITKEN

green books

First published in 2013 by
UIT / Green Books
PO Box 145, Cambridge CB4 1GQ, UK
www.greenbooks.co.uk
+44 1223 302 041

Design by Jayne Jones

With the exception of the images listed on page 246,
all photographs are by the authors.

ISBN: 978 0 85784 112 4 (paperback)
ISBN: 978 0 85784 114 8 (ePub)
ISBN: 978 0 85784 128 5 (Kindle)
ISBN: 978 0 85784 113 1 (pdf)

Disclaimer:
Many things we eat as a matter of course are toxic to some degree if not eaten in the right way,
at the right time and with the right preparation. At the time of going to press, the advice and
information in this book are believed to be true and accurate, and if plants are eaten according
to the guidance given here they are safe. However, someone, somewhere is allergic to almost
anything, so if you are trying completely new plants to eat, try them in moderation to begin
with. The authors and publisher accept no liability for actions inspired by this book.

10 9 8 7 6 5 4 3 2 1

Contents

Acknowledgements

Thanks to Caroline – the book would not have been written without you!

Thank to all at Green Books, especially Amanda, Alethea, Bee, Jayne and John.

Most of all thanks to my family.

Martin

Thanks to Patrick Whitefield for guiding me on my permaculture path and being a great friend and mentor. Thanks to Dana Kapitulčinová for her advice on the fascinating habits of micro-organisms. Great thanks to Martin Crawford for being a pleasure to work with and a continuing inspiration to myself and many others. My continuing gratitude goes to my students, who always teach me as much as I teach them, and who sowed the seed of inspiration for this book. And my greatest appreciation to my husband, Doug, whose patience, support and encouragement made all of this possible.

Caroline

For my son, Robin, who was born during the writing of this book. *Caroline*

. . . and for forest gardeners everywhere.

Introduction

This book is the result of a growing realisation for both of us that there is a notable gap in the forest garden library. For many years, we have both been asked – by people on tours around the forest garden in Dartington, or by students on permaculture courses – about how to prepare and cook unusual forest garden crops. It seems that many people may be deterred from embarking upon this new and exciting way to grow food because they are unsure about how to make use of the unfamiliar crops in the kitchen.

So, in these pages, Martin's forest garden expertise has been combined with Caroline's culinary skills (and experimentation) to create simple, delicious and practical recipes for everyday use. Many of the recipes will seem very familiar, just featuring forest garden perennials in place of staple annuals. If you decide to create a forest garden, or if you have done so already, then it is of course essential that the produce can be incorporated into daily cooking, and thereby the forest garden incorporated into your daily life. This is how the garden and the gardener really thrive – in symbiosis.

This is a cookbook for gardeners, not a gardening book, so, apart from a brief introduction to the plant being used, and a picture of it, you won't find detailed plant information here; for this you should refer to *Creating a Forest Garden*. Not every single plant in that book has its own entry in this one, but all of them are included in Appendix 1, which gives general guidance on culinary usage.

The main recipe section, Part 2, is ordered by season, and contains recipes for cooking with fresh produce. Although located in the book according to their main season of harvest, many of the plants are available for longer: Appendix 2 indicates the range of months within which each plant in Part 2 can be used. Part 1 comprises chapters on harvesting methods, drying and traditional preserving, including fermentation. For each preservation technique we give a brief explanation of the general method and some sample recipes. There are numerous books devoted to traditional preserving techniques – jams, chutneys, pickles, and so on. Fermenting is a less familiar technique for many people, but a wealth of information can be found in the books listed in the Resources section.

Drying is a fascinating way of preserving foods, especially fruits, and is also unfamiliar to many. In a damp climate, sun drying is not very viable, so extra heat has to be applied using a powered dehydrator, the results of which are superb. Information on the range of equipment available for food drying, along with the various other pieces of equipment described in Part 1, can be found in the Resources section.

A note on units: these are given in both metric and imperial, but note that the pint and fluid ounce values are UK units, which differ slightly from US units. 1 UK fl oz is in fact approximately equal to 1 US fl oz, while 1 UK pint is approximately equal to 1.2 US pints.

HARVESTING AND PRESERVING

CHAPTER 1

Harvesting

Given the busy lives that many of us lead today, it is important to be able to harvest our food crops quickly and efficiently. There are some simple and easy tips to speed up harvesting, which are described here.

Spring ground shoots

Examples include: Solomon's seal, ostrich fern, bamboo.

Ground shoots emerge in the spring, usually very fast. Once they start, you should check at least twice a week for the new tender shoots to harvest.

With most shoots, cutting cleanly with a knife at ground level is easiest and quickest. Small shoots like ostrich fern can be snapped off by hand. With some shoots, like bamboo shoots, a longer shoot can be obtained by digging down and cutting some centimetres below ground, although it's not always clear that it's worth the work involved.

Ostrich fern shoots.

Leaves

Examples include: lime, chicory, mulberries.

There is a lot to be said for tearing leaves off plants when harvesting, rather than trying to pick them neatly by cutting or breaking the leaf stalk. It is much faster to tear them off, but it does not leave the plants looking neat and tidy! However, tearing is how most herbivores harvest leaves, and it is what most plants are adapted to – by tearing you do not break into the leaf cells but tear along lines of cells. As a result, the leaves do not wilt or brown so quickly, and the remnant left on the tree is not so susceptible to fungal diseases entering the leaf or stalk. Hence it is better all round!

Of course, many chefs also recommend tearing leaves in salads rather than chopping them – for the same reason as described above. However, if you are going to eat the salad quickly then it probably makes no real difference.

Fruits

Fruits from trees and shrubs are likely to be major crops in most people's forest gardens, so knowing the most efficient way to harvest them is vital.

Large high fruits

Examples include: plums, pears, apples – on larger trees.

There are two sensible options here. One is to use a telescopic fruit picker – these have a harvesting head with a kind of crenulated edge and cloth bag to catch the fruit. Once you have got the hang of them they can be relatively fast and you can harvest several fruit at once. It is quickest if you harvest with a second person, so you can lower the picker and allow them to empty the bag.

The other option is not to harvest high fruits from the tree at all, but rather from the ground. For this to be practical you need to use the fruits immediately, as they will bruise within hours of harvesting. Making juice from them is one obvious possibility, and of course cider apples and perry pears are always harvested from the ground.

To harvest from the ground you need to make sure the ground cover beneath the tree (grass or whatever) is cut short before the fruit drops. When most of the fruit has dropped (often after a storm) you can shake or tap the branches to encourage any last fruits down before you harvest. You can just pick them up by hand, but it's much easier to use an 'Apple Wizard' hand harvester. You roll this over the ground, and the fruits 'ping' inside the wire cage. When it's full, you empty it into a bucket by twisting it on a special attachment fixed to the bucket. It's very quick and saves your back a lot of strain!

Smaller fruits

Examples include: autumn olives, rosehips, currants.

There are various options for fast harvesting. Some fruit fall well when the branches are shaken – hawthorn fruits (haws) are a good example. For these it is best to lay out a sheet or tarpaulin beneath the tree or bush and shake branches of the whole thing vigorously when the fruits are fully ripe. Harvesting takes just a few minutes, though of course there will be a few leaves, spiders, etc. to remove from the fruits.

For small fruits that are borne within reach on reasonably long fruit stalks, a harvesting 'comb' (or 'berry picker') is a good investment. These are small plastic or wooden hand-held tools with which you comb the fruits off a bush. They're good for currants, chokeberries, etc. If the fruits are not fully ripe, the comb will often pull off

Freshly harvested rosehips.

some stalk too, and you will have to sort through and remove these after harvest.

Some fruits are borne so densely – autumn olive is a good example – that it speeds things up considerably to hold a harvesting container beneath the branch with one hand while picking and dropping fruit with the other. Or you can put a sheet or tarp down on the ground and pick and drop straight down on to it.

Nuts

Examples include: chestnuts, heartnuts, walnuts.

Nuts are nearly always harvested off the ground after they drop from the tree. To make locating and harvesting efficient, you usually need to ensure that the ground cover beneath the trees (grass or whatever) is cut short just before the nuts drop and are harvested.

Nuts should be harvested from the ground as frequently as possible – preferably daily. Nuts on the ground are susceptible to predation and to

Harvesting walnuts using a Nut Wizard.

spiny burrs intact, and on a small scale the only practical way to deal with these is to open them by hand, using gloves thick enough to prevent the prickles getting your hands.

Most of the mainstream nuts fall free of their husks, but some of the unusual ones may need further processing to remove them. Heartnuts are a case in point – these always fall still encased in their greenish husks. We harvest them with Nut Wizards, then, after some days, the husks start to blacken and become soft – at this stage they go into a concrete mixer(!) with a few stones and some water. After a few minutes the mixture is turned out and the heartnuts are cleaned and free of husk, and just needing drying.

Tubers

Examples include: mashua, oca, yams.

There is no quick way of harvesting these, you just have to dig! If they are perennial tubers, remember to leave some in the ground to regrow.

Mushrooms

Examples include: oyster mushrooms, shiitake.

Mushrooms on logs can be picked by twisting or cutting off – it seems to make no difference to cropping either way. Harvest shiitake mushrooms on logs before they are fully open – ideally about the time the veil that protects the gills has just separated from the stem, or a day or two after. If you leave them too long the flavour will have peaked, they may become tougher, and the risk of mushroom fly larvae invading the mushroom increases dramatically (you don't really need the extra protein from these, as shiitake are already high in protein!).

picking up nut-rotting fungi. In particular, squirrels are a big problem in many areas. It helps if, prior to harvesting each day, you can shake or knock the branches to bring down any loose nuts still in the tree.

We now use 'Nut Wizard' harvesters to harvest most of our nuts. These are incredibly efficient hand-held tools: like the 'Apple Wizard', they have a wire-cage head which you roll over the ground; the nuts are gathered inside the head, then emptied into a bucket. There are different-sized Wizards for hazelnuts, chestnuts and walnuts. Some chestnuts always fall with their

CHAPTER 2

Traditional preserves

There are many books wholly devoted to the methods of preserving fruits and vegetables in sugar, vinegar or alcohol – namely, making jams, jellies, fruit 'cheeses', chutneys and vinegar or alcohol infusions. In this chapter, then, we are simply attempting to show how simple these methods are and how easily they are applied to almost any fruit or vegetable crop.

Jams

In jams (and jellies and fruit 'cheeses'), fruits are preserved by mixing with enough sugar to prevent mould growth and fermentation. Too little sugar and the jam will start to mould in store; too much and you will end up with an over-sweetened, insipid product, similar to many commercial jams.

Most jam recipes add too much sugar. Martin's basic jam recipe uses 50 per cent fruit, 50 per cent sugar by weight, and this leads to flavourful products that keep well before they are opened. However, after opening you need to keep them in a fridge or use them within a few weeks, otherwise moulds will start to grow on the surface. Jams with higher sugar levels than this will store for longer in ambient air temperatures once they are opened.

The fruit in jams needs cooking to break down the skins and make the fruit pulpy. Ideally, in jam making the fruit should be cooked for as little time as possible. It helps a lot if you make small batches of jam – a couple of kilos (about 4$\frac{1}{2}$lb) at a time is best – because the fruits cook very quickly and the jam itself takes only 20-30 minutes to make and bottle, so you can easily fit it in between other kitchen jobs.

It is preferable to use a heavy-bottomed stainless steel pan for making jams, chutneys and so on, as this transfers heat evenly and reduces the risk of sticking.

High- and low-pectin fruits

Some fruits (see below) are low in pectin and do not set easily as a jam. Pectin therefore needs to be added to the mixture, which is easiest to do in one of two ways:

- Add some chopped cooking apples to the fruit at the beginning. You need about one large apple per kilo (2lb 3oz) of fruit. Many cooking apples turn to a pulp when cooked and disappear into the jam; if they do not, you might want to put any lumpy bits through a Moulinex sieve.
- You can add pectin (which is extracted from apples), which you can buy in bottles. One bottle (250ml / 8¾fl oz) should suffice for 2kg (4lb 6oz) of fruit. Add the pectin after adding the sugar and bringing to the boil.

Apples are not the only fruit high in pectin, however – the other alternatives listed here can also be used in combination with low-pectin fruits to avoid adding bought pectin.

High in pectin: cooking apples, crab apples, currants, gooseberries, quince and flowering quinces, sour plums and damsons.
Low in pectin: autumn olives, blackberries, elderberries, medlars, pears, rhubarb, sea buckthorn, strawberries, haws and rosehips.

General method for jams

You can use the following method for virtually any fruit. Try mixing different fruits to make your own unique jams.

If the fruit is your own and clean, there is no need to wash it; just weigh and place in a pan. Bought fruit should be washed and weighed.

Add the minimum amount of water necessary to enable you to heat the pan and break down the fruit without it sticking to the bottom of the pan: how much depends how juicy the fruit is. With currants, for example, you can add around 5mm (1/8") depth of water for 1-2kg (approx. 2-4 1/2 lb) of fruit; autumn olive needs more – around 1-1.5cm (3/8-5/8") depth for 2kg (4lb 6oz) of fruit.

Bring the fruit to the boil and cook just until the skins are well broken – 5 to 10 minutes should be enough – and stir well throughout to stop the fruit sticking and to ensure it is all cooked.

If you are making a jam from fruits with large seeds, for example haws, then the seeds should be removed now. Put the cooked fruit mixture through a Moulinex sieve to remove seeds and leave the pulp. Weigh the pulp again to determine the amount of sugar needed.

Next, add the sugar. Any kind of sugar can be used – brown granulated sugar is fine and is less refined than white sugar. Preserving sugar has large sugar crystals, which reduce the risk of burning and therefore the need for stirring constantly. Most sugar comes from either sugar beet or sugar cane; the former grown in temperate climes and the latter, of course, in the tropics. You might think that the local sugar is more 'eco', but that is not necessarily the case. Martin's own energy analysis of the two crops shows that more energy is used in the growing, processing and transport of sugar beet than in sugar cane. See box, right, for a discussion of sugar alternatives.

Add the same weight of sugar as you had of fruit to begin with (or of the pulp if you have removed seeds) for a 50:50 jam. Bring back to the boil and boil vigorously (called a rolling boil) for several minutes. Meanwhile, put a small ceramic plate in the fridge to cool down.

After a few minutes of boiling, and every few minutes afterwards if necessary, test the jam to see if it will set. If the jam is bottled before it is ready to set, then it will be runny (although still usable). Get out your now-cold plate from the fridge and drop a quarter of a teaspoon of the cooking jam on to it. Blow on it to help it cool. After a minute or so it will have cooled sufficiently for you to push the little pool of jam with your finger. If it has set, the skin on the jam surface will ruck up and wrinkle. If it has not set, the pool will just flow where you push it.

Once the jam is setting, take it off the heat immediately and pour into jars (see box opposite) with a jam funnel. It is far better to use screw-top jars than to try to cover jams with waxed paper, as it

Alternatives to sugar in jams

Some folk dislike the use of refined sugar; however, unfortunately there is no simple alternative to using sugar in jams. Various substitutes can be used, but they all have disadvantages of one sort or another.

- Honey: works well but gives you honey-flavoured jams of course! It is also expensive unless the honey is your own.
- Concentrated fruit juices: apple juice and grape juice can be used, but if you are starting with fresh juices they need concentrating by boiling off the water for a significant time. This ends up being very expensive, and, as with honey, the flavour of the jam can be affected.
- Stevia (either powdered leaf or a processed stevia product): although this sweetens, it is not a preservative. If you make a jam using stevia you will need to treat the jars in the same way as for bottling tomatoes, for example – i.e. cook filled but unsealed jars in an oven to ensure sterilisation before sealing. There is a real risk of botulism unless proper procedures are followed.

Salal fruits in August make a fine jam. Add just 5mm (⅛") depth of water or so for cooking 1kg (2lb 3oz) of fruit. You'll spot a couple of blueberries in the pan in the photo, which happened to be spare and which complement salal well.

Sterilising, bottling and storage of preserves

All containers (and lids) used for storing preserves should be sterilised.

To sterilise glass jars, place in an oven at 100°C (212°F / Gas Mark ¼) for 20 minutes. Alternatively, you can submerge them in boiling water for 5 minutes. Jar lids should be boiled, as the rubber seals may melt in the oven. Screw-top lids are best. When bottling jams and jellies, the jars should be hot, as cold glass may break on contact with boiling-hot jam (which is hotter than boiling water).

It helps to fill jars to the brim in order to exclude as much air as possible, as this will reduce the likelihood of mould forming on the surface. Surface mould can form after the jars are opened, even in the fridge, but it can just be skimmed off with a spoon. For runny preserves, a jam funnel helps.

Screw the lids on firmly. It is a good idea to ensure that lids are hot, as this helps to ensure a tight seal.

You can stand the jars upside down for a couple of minutes to sterilise the air space below the lid. If you don't have lids with plastic or rubber seals, place a film of plastic (e.g. a cut-out circle of plastic carrier bag) between the lid and the jar. Vinegar-based preserves can corrode the metal over time, even if the lids do have rubber seals.

Once your jars are sealed, remember to label the containers clearly with the contents and date, to avoid confusion later in the year when the store cupboard is full of different-coloured jars. It is particularly important to be able to distinguish last year's preserves from this year's. Preserves should keep for at least a year, but it's always good practice to eat the oldest ones first. Store in a cool, dark place.

Once opened, jams, jellies, cheeses and chutneys should be kept in the fridge. Vinegar and alcohol infusions do not need to be refrigerated.

will keep much better. As a general rule, a couple of kilos of jam (1kg of fruit and 1kg of sugar) fills about six 400ml (14fl oz) jars.

Store somewhere cool if possible, and remember to label the jars with the contents and the date. However hard one tries, a two-year-old jar of jam always seems to lurk unnoticed at the back of the cupboard – at least if it's labelled you can identify it!

Jellies

Jelly is essentially jam without the bits! In order to get a clear jelly, more water is added to the fruit while cooking and the watery pulp is then passed through a jelly bag to extract the juice. Jelly bags are made of a thicker fabric than muslin, to ensure a really clear juice, and the process is slow. Traditionally the bag would be hung between the legs of an upturned stool to drip into a saucepan overnight – you could hang it from a door handle if you don't have a rustic milking stool to hand! It is good practice to boil the jelly bag before and after use to prevent it mouldering in storage.

Many traditional jellies use some kind of wild berry combined with apples or crab apples to add pectin. Examples include rowan jelly and rosehip jelly. Currants – for example, redcurrants for

redcurrant jelly – are high in pectin and therefore don't need apples added to them. See the box on page 17 for some high- and low-pectin fruits that may be combined.

The basic ratios to use in making jelly are given in the box below left. Caroline's recipe for haw jelly, below, follows these guidelines.

General method for jellies

Once the juice has been extracted, the cooking method is the same as for jam (see page 18): bring the juice to the boil in a large, heavy-based saucepan, stir in the sugar and cook on a rolling boil until the jelly is ready to set. Test this using the cold plate test, then carefully transfer to hot sterilised jars with screw-top lids. Remember to label the jars with the date and contents.

Jelly-making ratios

- 1 part whole low-pectin fruit : 1 part whole high-pectin fruit
- 1l (1¾ pints) water : 2kg (4lb 6oz) fruit (variable depending on the juiciness of the fruit)
- Same volume of sugar as extracted juice – as described in the haw jelly recipe, right (roughly 450g/1lb sugar to 570ml/1 pint juice)

Haw jelly

Makes about 6-8 x 400ml (14fl oz) jars

1kg (2lb 3oz) haws

1kg (2lb 3oz) cooking apples

1l (1¾ pints) water

Granulated sugar (approx. 900g/2lb – see method)

Place the whole haws into a saucepan with 600ml (21fl oz) water and bring to the boil over a medium heat. Reduce the heat and simmer for 10 minutes or until the haws are pulpy. Remove from the heat and put to one side. Chop the apples into chunks (no need to peel or core) and place in a saucepan with 400ml (14fl oz) water. Bring to the boil and simmer for 5-10 minutes until pulped. Add the haws to the apples and stir well.

Find a safe place to hang your jelly bag and place a saucepan beneath it to collect the juice. Carefully pour the fruit into the jelly bag. Lots of juice will run out at first but will gradually slow to a drip. Leave the bag hanging overnight.

Measure out the extracted juice – you should have about 1.4l (2½ pints). Measure out the same volume of sugar as you have juice. It is easier to think in terms of volume than weight of sugar, as the amount of juice you extract can be quite variable and the important thing is to have equivalent volumes of juice and sugar.

Put the juice over a high heat and bring to the boil. Add the sugar and stir until it has dissolved. Keep the jelly at a rolling boil for 15 minutes, or until it has reached setting point (see the general method for jam, page 18). You may need to remove some froth from the surface of the jelly with a spoon. Transfer the jelly to sterilised jars, seal and label.

This jelly is delicious with roasted meats and with creamy French cheeses.

Try this recipe with rosehips or autumn olives instead of haws, or make a mixed fruit jelly with 1kg (2lb 3oz) mixed hips and berries and 1kg apples. You can also try crab apples instead of cooking apples.

Fruit 'cheeses'

Fruit 'cheeses' can be made with various tree fruits and are a great way to preserve some of an abundant harvest in a different way. They are not actually cheeses, of course, but firm fruit concentrates, somewhere between a jam and a fruit leather (for details of leathers, see page 35). They are also known as fruit paste or 'membrillo', and have been made traditionally in South America with fruits such as guava. They have perhaps been named 'cheeses' in the English-speaking world because they complement cheese very well and can be eaten with cheese and crackers, or as a sweet spread on bread.

General method for cheeses

A fruit cheese is a made in a very similar way to jam and jelly, but the aim is to create a firm paste which can either be spread or sliced, depending upon how firm you make it. Pears, medlars and haws make particularly good cheeses, as they create the right texture.

Place chopped large fruit or small whole fruit into a heavy-based saucepan and just cover with water. Boil the fruit until it forms a soft pulp, then sieve if necessary to remove cores, pips or skins.

Weigh the sieved pulp and return it to the pan. Weigh out the same measure (note: the same weight, not the same volume, in contrast to jellies) of granulated or preserving sugar and add that to the pulp. Add the juice and zest of one lemon to add pectin and enhance the flavour. Bring back to the boil, reduce to a simmer and stir regularly for between 1 and 3 hours. The length of time needed depends on how watery the pulp is and how thick you want your fruit cheese to be. The pulp will darken and thicken as it cooks and you will eventually be able to see the base of the pan for a second when you run the spoon across it.

You can use the cold plate test (as described in general method for jam, page 18) to check the consistency as you cook, and when it sets as thickly as you want it, pour the paste into sterilised jars, as with jam or jelly, or into moulds greased with butter, which can be turned out when the cheese is cool. Fruit cheeses in sterilised and sealed containers will keep for as long as jams and jellies, so label the jars or containers with the date and contents and enjoy throughout the year. If set in an open mould they will need to be refrigerated and eaten within a month.

Quince cheese

1kg (2lb 3oz) quinces, peeled, cored and diced
Granulated sugar (same weight as pulped fruit)
1 lemon, juice and zest
Water (see method)

Put the quinces into a large heavy-based saucepan and add water to just cover the fruit. Simmer on a low heat for about 20 minutes until soft.

Drain off the water and weigh the fruit. Note the weight of the fruit and weigh out the same measure of sugar. Put the quinces into a blender to make a smooth purée, return it to the pan and add the sugar, lemon juice and zest.

Bring the mixture to the boil, stirring continuously until the sugar has dissolved. Turn the hob down as low as possible and allow the pulp to simmer gently for up to 3 hours or until the mixture is so thick that you can see the bottom of the pan when you run your spoon across it. You will need to keep an eye on the pan, stirring regularly to stop it burning on the bottom and to ensure that it reduces evenly.

When the mixture is ready it will be a deep caramel colour and very thick and sticky with a slightly grainy texture. Spoon into sterilised jars to store for up to a year, or into a pudding basin to be served when it has cooled and set. To turn it out of the basin, dip a palette knife into hot water and run it around the edge between the bowl and the set cheese, then put a plate on top and turn it upside down. The cheese should pop out on to the plate.

Chutneys

In chutneys, vinegar is the agent of preservation, although some sugar is usually added to offset the acidity of the vinegar. Almost any mixture of vegetables and fruits can be preserved in this way, and will store for several years if required, although of course some nutrients will decline after a year or so. Chutneys are a great complement to cheeses, cold meats and Indian food.

General method for chutneys

The evening before you are going to cook the chutney, chop the vegetables and fruits into smallish pieces (around 1cm/½" or smaller) and place in a large heavy-based pan. Add salt and spices, mix well and leave overnight for the salt to draw out some of the juices.

The following day, add sugar and vinegar. The vinegar quality has a great bearing on the quality of the final product, so try to use wine or cider vinegar. You will want about 100g (3½oz) sugar and about 140ml (¼ pint) vinegar per 1kg (2lb 3oz) of vegetables/fruits.

Bring to the boil and simmer, uncovered, for 2 hours. Stir more often as the cooking progresses and the liquid reduces, to make sure the chutney does not stick to the bottom of the pan. The chutney will thicken as it cooks, and when it's ready you should be able to part the mixture with a spoon and see the bottom of the pan for a couple of seconds before the mixture closes back over it.

Bottle in hot sterilised jars (see page 19). The flavour of chutney matures over time and it is best to leave it for at least 2 months before eating. Label the jars clearly with the contents and date.

Spicy plum chutney

This is a great way to use up a surplus of cooking plums or damsons in late summer or early autumn.

Makes about 20 x 400ml (14fl oz) jars

1.5kg (3lb 5oz) cooking apples, cored and peeled
500g (1lb 2oz) onions
2.5kg (5lb 8oz) plums or damsons, stoned
50g (1¾oz) coriander seeds
1½ tbsp salt
25g (1oz) ground ginger
Juice of 1 lemon
500g (1lb 2oz) sugar

4 tbsp golden syrup
700ml (25fl oz) cider vinegar
500g (1lb 2oz) sultanas

Chop the apples, onions and plums, and add the coriander, salt and ginger. Mix well and leave overnight.

The next day, add the remaining ingredients, bring the mixture to the boil and simmer for 2 hours, stirring occasionally to prevent burning on the bottom. When you can part the mixture with a spoon and see the bottom of the pan for a couple of seconds, the mixture is ready.

Spoon into sterilised jars, seal and label. If using metal lids, use a film of plastic between the lid and the jar to prevent the metal from corroding.

Flowering quince & haw chutney

Flowering quinces are much smaller than culinary varieties and can be more fiddly to prepare. You may find it easiest to halve or quarter them and scoop out the large seeds with a fingertip or the tip of a butter knife. If the fruit is ripe, the seeds and pith should come out easily and quickly. If you have large quantities to process you needn't de-seed the fruit first, as the seeds can be removed by sieving the pulp after cooking, but as there are so many seeds this too can be time-consuming.

This recipe uses small quantities, as the fruits are small and take some preparation. If you do have larger quantities you can simply double or triple the quantities listed here.

Makes 800ml (roughly 1½ pints), or 2 x 400ml (14fl oz) jars, of chutney

400g (14oz) japonica quince purée, pulped and sieved

300g (10½oz) haw purée, pulped and sieved

300g (10½oz) onion, finely chopped

100g (3½oz) raisins

3 cloves of garlic, crushed

5cm (2") piece fresh ginger, peeled and grated

170ml (6fl oz) vinegar

140g (5oz) brown sugar

¼ tsp ground cardamom

¼ tsp ground cinnamon

¼ tsp ground chilli

¼ tsp ground black pepper

For the quince purée: Place the quince pieces into a saucepan with a little water and simmer gently for up to 10 minutes. If you have not removed the seeds first, sieve the pulp after cooking. 500g (1lb 2oz) of fruit with 150ml (5¼fl oz) water will produce around 400g (14oz) of purée.

For the haw purée: Gently cook the haws whole over a low heat for around 15 minutes. If they are fairly hard, add half an inch of water to the pan and cover. Remove from the heat. Once cooled, mash with a potato masher or a pestle to split the skins and release the haw pulp. Transfer to a large sieve and use a pestle or a wooden spoon to push the pulp through the sieve into a bowl, a spoonful at a time, discarding the skin and seeds as you go (alternatively, use a Moulinex sieve – see page 163). 500g (1lb 2oz) of haws with 150ml (5¼fl oz) water will produce around 300g (10½oz) purée.

Place all ingredients into large, heavy-based, stainless steel pan and slowly bring to the boil over a medium heat, stirring regularly. Leave the pan uncovered and allow to simmer gently for about 2 hours, stirring occasionally to prevent burning on the bottom.

When you can part the mixture with a spoon and see the bottom of the pan for a couple of seconds, the chutney is ready. Spoon into sterilised jars, seal and label. If using metal lids, use a film of plastic between the lid and the jar to prevent the metal from corroding.

Vinegar preserves

The pickled foods we buy in shops are usually pasteurised vinegar pickles, i.e. they have been placed in vinegar to preserve them. From British pickled onions to Chinese artichoke pickles, this technique is widespread and enduring – and very simple. Vinegar, which is itself a product of fermentation, may also be used for preserving foods by fermentation (see Chapter 4) and some pickles are made this way. However, shop-bought vinegar has lost its microbial life during the pasteurisation process, so when used to make vinegar preserves, any additional health benefits associated with fermentation do not apply. But the intense and diverse flavours that can be achieved are worth exploring, and the better the quality of the vinegar, the more refined the end product will be.

Pickled Chinese artichokes

In China and Japan, Chinese artichoke pickles are a popular snack. They come processed, packaged and dyed pink! This recipe offers a more humble, home-made version, which enables you to enjoy this delicate, crunchy tuber all year round.

200g (7oz) Chinese artichokes

1 garlic clove

1 whole dried chilli

2.5cm (1") piece fresh ginger, finely sliced

1 tsp course sea salt

1 tsp fennel seeds

250ml (8¾fl oz) water

250ml (8¾fl oz) rice vinegar

Note: The measurements given here are for a 750ml (26fl oz) jar, but the quantity of liquid should always be two-thirds the volume of the jar to allow for displacement. The ratio of liquid is always 1 part vinegar to 1 part water.

Put the garlic, chilli, ginger, salt and fennel into the bottom of the jar. Fill the jar with whole artichokes to within 2-3 centimetres (an inch) of the top, allowing for the contents to swell a little over time.

Measure out the water and vinegar and add them to a saucepan. Bring the liquid to the boil and turn off the heat. Pour the liquid into the jar until about a centimetre (half an inch) from the top and replace the lid. Have a deep saucepan ready, half full of boiling water, transfer the sealed jar to the pan and boil for 10 minutes.

Remove the jar from the pan and allow to cool. Label it with the ingredients and the date and allow to mature for 2 months before eating. This allows the flavours to infuse and the vinegar to mellow.

Vinegar infusions

Vinegar infusions are made by steeping various fruits, vegetables or herbs in vinegar to add flavour to it. In Italy, garlic, chillies and herbs are traditionally infused in white wine vinegar and used to make salad dressings. Likewise, in Japan, rice wine is infused with herbs and spices and used in cooking.

Szechuan-infused rice vinegar

3 heads of Szechuan peppercorns
3 fennel leaves
1 elephant garlic clove, peeled
30g (1oz) fresh ginger, cut into strips
1l (1¾ pints) rice vinegar

Place all ingredients except the vinegar into the bottom of a 1l glass storage jar. Pour over the vinegar and seal the jar. If the jar has a metal lid, remember to use a film of plastic between the lid and the jar to prevent the metal from corroding.

Put the jar in a cool dark place, such as a cupboard, for a month. Strain the contents and transfer the vinegar to a sterilised, labelled bottle. Vinegar does not need to be refrigerated and will keep for months.

You can return a few peppercorns to the vinegar for decoration, or add fresh ones if you have them.

Other vinegar infusions

- Wineberries and lemon balm in plum vinegar (add to lemonade for a refreshing soft drink).
- Rosemary, thyme and garlic in white wine vinegar (add to salad dressings or pasta sauce).
- Sea buckthorn in cider vinegar (as a health tonic).
- Rowan berries, rosehips and haws in red wine vinegar (for use in casseroles and stews)
- Fennel and apple mint in white wine vinegar (to add to salad dressings).

Alcohol infusions

There is a long tradition in Britain and the USA of preserving leaves and berries in spirits with sugar to make syrupy sweet liqueurs. Perhaps the most popular in Britain is sloe gin, made from the deep purple berries of the blackthorn tree, while in the USA there is a growing number of devotees to beech leaf noyau, a milder gin-based tipple.

Tree leaves are at their most succulent and edible when they first unfurl in spring, and those such as hawthorn, beech and lime have a relatively small window for picking before they become too tough. The delicate flavours can then be captured and preserved for those long, dark months within a warming winter liqueur. Columbine leaves are less commonly used than beech leaves, but their sweet flavour lends itself well to the same process.

As the alcohol is itself a preservative, you can adjust the sugar levels to taste, as well as adding more or fewer leaves to vary the flavour.

Using a funnel, pour sugar into the bottles until it reaches around one-sixth of the way up.

Wash the leaves and dry them in a salad spinner or with a clean tea towel. Using the handle end of a wooden spoon, push the leaves into the bottles until they fill the bottle to roughly halfway up, making sure they are well packed in.

Top the bottles up with gin, screw the lids on tightly and give them all a gentle shake to loosen up the leaves and distribute the sugar. The liqueur will brew in the bottles over the course of 2-3 months, so label them with the date and turn them every so often to prevent settling and help with the infusion of the leaf flavours.

Beech or columbine gin liqueur

Approximate ratios (adjustable to taste):
1 part white granulated sugar
2 parts beech or columbine leaves
3 parts gin

You will need sterilised bottles at the ready, twice the capacity of the quantity of gin you have (e.g. for 1 litre of gin you'll need a 2-litre bottle).

Other spirit infusions

- Wineberries, raspberries, blackberries or autumn olives in vodka.
- Apple mint, spearmint or other mints in Pernod.
- Hawthorn leaves and fruits in brandy.
- Lemon balm or apple mint in gin or vodka.

CHAPTER 3

Drying fruit and nuts

Dried foods have been used for survival from the times of early nomadic people to the modern day. The ancient Egyptians and Greeks used this method, and early sea-going expeditions survived on dried fruit, grains and meats. Until recent times in many parts of the world, food drying was a necessity anywhere where homes had to be self-reliant during cold and unproductive winter months.

The culture of food drying has been strongest in parts of the world where hot, sunny days in summer and autumn are the norm and can be relied upon for solar drying techniques to be used successfully. Leafy parts of plants and herbs are easy enough to dry in most climates without additional heat, but to dry fruits – which are dense and consist largely of water – you need higher temperatures. In climates such as those of northern Europe, therefore, solar drying by itself is rarely sufficient.

The first dehydrator used to dry fruits and vegetables by artificial means was employed in France in 1795, to dry thinly sliced vegetables and fruits. It used a continuous hot air flow at 40°C (104°F). Drying on a large scale was not used until the First World War, then again in the Second World War, when tremendous quantities of dried foods were needed to feed troops in the field. Considerable research on food drying took place at these times. Today, dried fruit production is a huge industry.

See 'Drying methods', page 40, for information on dehydrators and other means of drying.

Drying principles

There are two things needed to efficiently dry (dehydrate) fruits, nuts and other plant material:
- warm air
- air circulation.

Warmth alone is not sufficient, as the still air soon becomes saturated with moisture from the plant material. Air circulation alone is also not usually sufficient. If only one of the two requirements is in place, in a climate such as that of the UK, the result is either a cool moist atmosphere or a warm moist atmosphere, which encourages fungal rots – which can very quickly ruin crops. When drying plant material, the clock is ticking, and if you do not dry fast enough the food is compromised by starting to ferment, starting to rot or losing nutrients.

The moisture-carrying capacity of the air is dependent on the temperature. Each 15°C (27°F) increase in temperature doubles the moisture-carrying capacity of the air. If the temperature is too hot, the food will case-harden, i.e. form a hard shell that traps moisture inside and slows down further drying.

Some fruits are not well suited to drying because of their very high water content and therefore slow drying rate – for example, blackcurrants and redcurrants; these are better preserved in other ways. A few fruits, such as blackberries and raspberries, are very seedy and if dried the seeds are emphasised – so these too are best not dried.

Drying fruits

Drying fruits is an excellent way to deal with a glut that you cannot deal with in its fresh state, which is a common occurrence with tree and bush fruit that has been bred for the crop to ripen over a short period.

Preparation

The best-quality dried fruit comes from fruit at the peak of ripeness, so do not pick under-ripe or overripe fruit. Try to avoid picking for drying just after heavy rain or irrigation, as this increases moisture levels in the fruit. Make sure the fruit is picked carefully and kept clean. If necessary (for example, if any fruits have been picked off the ground) wash fruits in cold water to remove soil, bacteria and insect larvae just before processing.

Most fruits do not need to be peeled before drying, although peeled fruit will dry more quickly. But for most fruits to dry quickly enough to prevent spoilage, the skin has to be opened up in some way to allow the moisture to escape. Use sharp stainless steel knives for cutting. This can be done in various ways, as follows.

Pitting Small fruits with a pit or stone, such as cherries, should be pitted/stoned before drying: this shortens the drying time and produces a better-tasting fruit. Depending on the size of the fruit, they may need to be halved as well.

Halving or quartering Apricots, peaches and pears, for example, can be halved or quartered and the stone or core removed. They are then dried skin-side down to prevent the juices from dripping out and to retain flavour. Specific varieties, especially of plums, are called 'freestone' if the stone comes away freely when the fruit is halved. In 'clingstone' varieties the flesh adheres to the stone.

Flattening Soft-textured fruits, such as plums/prunes or apricots, can be flattened to shorten the drying time after halving and removing the stones – use your thumbs to press the rounded side in, which exposes more drying surface to the air.

Slicing Larger fruits, for example apples, should be peeled and cut into slices 0.5-1cm (1/8-3/8") thick. Uniform slices will dry at a consistent rate. With some fruits (e.g. peaches and pears), slicing lengthwise will give fewer, larger pieces than will slicing crosswise. A neat hand-cranked machine is available that will peel, slice and core apples all in one action. The spaghetti-like peel from these machines can itself be dried into apple crisps.

Blanching or checking Small fruits, such as blueberries, cherries and grapes, have a waxy bloom (a thin, natural wax-like coating) which keeps moisture in. Blanching or 'checking' this bloomy skin will decrease the drying time. Commercially, fruits are checked by dipping them in lye, which removes the waxy coating – a potentially dangerous process, since lye is a highly caustic substance. On a small scale, the fruits can be dipped whole into boiling water just long enough (up to a couple of minutes) to break the skins, since it's not possible to remove the wax itself with boiling water.

Pre-treatment

All fruits and vegetables contain enzymes and other chemicals that cause them to ripen. Drying slows the effect of these enzymes, but some continue to work even after the food (especially in the case of vegetables) has been dried, which can lead to poor rehydration and flavour. Some fruits tend to oxidise (i.e. combine with oxygen in the air) during drying and storage, which can cause loss of vitamins and flavour loss. Oxidation and enzyme reactions cause fruits, especially apples, pears, peaches and apricots, to turn brown when cut and exposed to air.

The action of enzymes can be stopped and oxidation minimised by pre-treating fruits after cutting. Place them in a 'holding' solution of ascorbic acid (Vitamin C), which is available from wine-making shops, for two minutes or more (but no longer than an hour). Use 1 teaspoon of ascorbic acid per litre of water. Lemon juice or citric acid can also be used, though these are not as effective and may add flavours to the fruit. Sulphur dioxide is often used commercially – also as a fungicide – but is not recommended because of possible adverse health effects. After removing from the solution, drain them off and blot dry with kitchen paper before placing in the dryer.

Dried pears

Drying is especially useful for summer and early autumn pears, which ripen all at once and have to be harvested all at the same time.

Cut pears into quarters and remove a small sliver of core from each quarter. Hold in ascorbic acid solution.

Lay them on trays, skin side against the tray, and dry at about 57°C (135°F) until leathery but still chewy – about 8-16 hours.

Store in airtight containers.

Dried pears are brown in colour and, it must be said, do not look the most inviting food to eat. But once you have tasted them you will be amazed at their fantastic intense flavour!

The drying process

Preheat the dryer (if you are using a dehydrator or other heated system) and arrange the prepared fruit on drying trays, leaving small spaces between slices or pieces for air circulation. Different fruits can be dried together, as they won't emit a strong odour. Dry fruit halves or slices of similar size on the same tray to reduce the need for sorting near the end of the drying process. Small fruits such as cherries should be stirred occasionally to promote even drying.

As far as possible, try not to interrupt the drying process. Do not add fresh moist pieces to a dryer filled with partially dried fruit – the increased humidity will greatly increase the drying time of the pieces that are partly dry.

Dried plums

Dried plums are delicious, and this is a good way to use up an excess. It is best to use a freestone variety (see 'Halving or quartering', opposite). The photo above shows the early cherry plum 'Golden Sphere'.

Halve the plums and remove the stones.

Lay them on trays, skin side against the tray, and dry at about 57°C (135°F) until leathery but still chewy – about 22-30 hours.

Store in airtight containers.

Suggested drying temperatures and times are listed in the table on page 33. Most fruits dry best at about 57°C (135°F). Either dry at this temperature throughout, or use initial drying temperatures of up to 60°C (140°F) for 1-3 hours to remove surface moisture quickly, before reducing the temperature to 55-57°C (131-135°F).

The ideal moisture content of home-dried fruits should be 15-20 per cent – some moisture is needed for a chewy texture if fruits are to be eaten dried. This moisture content is lower than in commercially dried fruits, which are dried to 30-35 per cent moisture, then treated with fungicides such as sulphur dioxide.

Test the fruits frequently near the end of the drying process to avoid over-drying them. The easiest dryness test is touching and tasting! The cooled fruit should be chewy and leather-like with no moisture pockets. See box, right, for how to measure moisture content more accurately.

Conditioning

When drying has been achieved, some pieces will be moister than others because of the irregular size of the pieces or their location in the dryer. 'Conditioning' is a process used to distribute the residual moisture evenly in the fruit. It reduces the chance of spoilage, particularly from moulds.

After the dried fruit has cooled, loosely pack it in plastic or glass containers to about two-thirds full. Seal tightly and let them stand for 2-4 days at room temperature. The excess moisture in some pieces will be absorbed by the drier pieces. Shake the containers daily to separate the pieces and check for signs of condensation – if this occurs, further drying is required. Conditioning can take place in the final storage container, or the fruit can be repacked after conditioning.

Maintenance of dryers

Drying trays should be scrubbed clean at regular intervals to stop the growth of moulds on them, which can spoil fruit.

The inside of dryers should also be cleaned at least once a season. Fruits can sometimes drip, and fruit leathers (see page 35) occasionally leak over the edge of the trays.

Calculating moisture loss and final weight

You can calculate the dryness of fruit accurately by weighing the fruits when fresh and dry, and referring to the moisture content values in the table opposite. In general, aim for a finished moisture content of 15-20% unless the table indicates otherwise. For example, if you were drying apricots:

- From the table, apricots contain approximately 85% water by weight.
- Weigh a single tray of the halved, pitted apricots. As an example: 1.0kg (1000g)
- Calculate the total weight of water in the apricots: 1.0 x 0.85 = 0.85kg
- Calculate the weight of water to be removed; in this example to achieve 20% moisture (i.e. losing 80% or 0.8 of the water): 0.85 x 0.8 = 0.68kg (680g)
- The weight of the apricots when dried should be the initial weight minus the water removed: 1000-680 = 320g

So, weigh the apricots frequently towards the end of the drying process until this weight has been achieved.

Storage

Dried fruits should be packed in plastic bags or glass jars with minimal air. Package in small amounts that can be used up within a few days of opening. Seal bags with a heat sealer or heavy rubber bands and store smaller bags inside large plastic or metal containers.

If there is a risk that fruits still have insect larvae in them (for example, if you often get maggoty

Drying advice for common fruits				
Fruit	Water content (by weight)	Preparation	Drying*	Dryness test / comments
Apples	84%	Peel, core and slice into 7mm (¼") slices or rings. Hold in ascorbic acid solution.	57°C (135°F) for 7-15 hours; or 65°C (149°F) for 2-3 hours, then 55°C (131°F) until dry (10% moisture).	Pliable to crisp. Best varieties are firm-textured dessert varieties on the sharp side.
Apricots	85%	Halve and remove stones. Hold in ascorbic acid solution.	57°C (135°F) for 20-28 hours; or 70°C (158°F) for 2-3 hours, then 55°C (131°F) until dry.	Pliable with no pockets of moisture.
Blueberries	83%	Remove stems. Dip in boiling water to remove bloom.	57°C (135°F) for 6-10 hours; or 65°C (149°F) for 2-3 hours, then 55°C (131°F) until dry.	Leathery and pliable with no pockets of moisture.
Cherries	84% (sour); 80% (sweet)	Remove stems, halve (optional) and remove stone; place skin-side down.	57°C (135°F) for 13-21 hours; or 70°C (158°F) for 2-3 hours, then 55°C (131°F) until dry.	Leathery and pliable with no pockets of moisture. Sweet varieties are nicest.
Cranberries	88%	Dip in boiling water to remove bloom.	57°C (135°F) for 10-12 hours; or 60°C (140°F) until dry (5% moisture).	Shrivelled, pliable, sticky. Best combined with other dry fruits.
Figs	78%	Remove stems, halve or (for large fruits) quarter. Dry skin-side down.	57°C (135°F) for 22-30 hours; or 70°C (158°F) for 1-2 hours, then 55°C (131°F) until dry.	Leathery and pliable with no pockets of moisture.
Grapes	81%	Whole or halved, skin-side down. Blanching will reduce drying times given here by 50%.	57°C (135°F) for 22-30 hours, or 70°C (158°F) for 1-2 hours, then 55°C (131°F) until dry.	Leathery and pliable with no pockets of moisture. Use only seedless varieties. Produces raisins.
Kiwi fruits	82%	Remove skin and slice into 7mm (¼") slices.	60°C (140°F) for 7-15 hours until dry.	Leathery and pliable with no pockets of moisture.
Mulberries	90%	Remove stalks.	57°C (135°F) for 7-15 hours, or 65°C (149°F) for 1-2 hours, then 55°C (131°F) until dry.	Leathery and pliable.
Nectarines	82%	Halve, remove stone, cut into quarters and dry skin-side down, or cut into 1cm (⅜") slices. Hold in ascorbic acid solution.	57°C (135°F) for 8-16 hours; or 70°C (158°F) for 2-3 hours, then 55°C (131°F) until dry.	Leathery and pliable with no pockets of moisture.

* To 15-20% moisture unless otherwise indicated.

(Cont.)

33

		Drying advice for common fruits		
Fruit	Water content (by weight)	Preparation	Drying*	Dryness test / comments
Peaches	89%	Scald for a few seconds to remove skins. Cut into 1cm (⅜") slices. Hold in ascorbic acid solution.	57°C (135°F) for 8-16 hours; or 65°C (149°F) for 2-3 hours, then 55°C (131°F) until dry.	Leathery and pliable with no pockets of moisture. Clingstone varieties dry better than freestone ones.
Pears (European)	83%	Peel thinly, core and cut into 7mm (¼") slices. Hold in ascorbic acid solution.	57°C (135°F) for 8-16 hours; or 70°C (158°F) for 2-3 hours, then 55°C (131°F) until dry.	Leathery and pliable with no pockets of moisture. Summer pears such as 'Williams' are best.
Pears (Asian)	81%	Peel, core and cut into 12mm (½") slices.	60°C (140°F) until dry.	Leathery and pliable with no pockets of moisture. All varieties good.
Persimmons	79%	Remove stem cap, halve and then cut into 7mm (¼") slices.	60°C (140°F) for 1-2 hours, then 55°C (131°F) for 10-16 hours until dry.	Light-to-medium brown; tender and pliable but not sticky.
Plums	81%	Halve and remove stone, then cut into 7-10mm (¼-⅜") slices, leaving peel intact, or pop the backs and flatten.	57°C (135°F) for 22-30 hours; or 70°C (158°F) for 1-2 hours, then 55°C (131°F) until dry (18% moisture).	Leathery and pliable. Freestone varieties are much easier to prepare than clingstone ones.
Rhubarb	93%	Wash and cut into 2.5cm (1") lengths	57°C (135°F) for 6-10 hours.	Leathery.
Strawberries	90%	Remove cap, cut into 7mm (¼") slices or halve if small (dry skin-side down).	57°C (135°F) for 7-15 hours; or 65°C (149°F) for 1-2 hours, then 55°C (131°F) until dry.	Leathery and pliable with no pockets of moisture. Firm varieties dry best.

* To 15-20% moisture unless otherwise indicated.

apples from your tree), dried fruits can be freeze-pasteurised by placing in a freezer set below -20°C (-4°F) for 2-14 days. This will kill any larvae still alive in the dried fruits.

The storage life of dried fruits depends on a number of factors:
- Residual moisture. Most fruits are dried to 15-20 per cent of their moisture. If they contain too much they will rot. Too little moisture, on the other hand, makes them unpalatable and causes large nutrient losses.
- Storage temperature. The lower the temperature, the longer dried foods will remain in prime condition. Temperatures below 16°C (61°F) will maintain most dried foods in good condition for about a year. At 27°C (81°F) or more, they will start to deteriorate after several months. For every decrease of 10°C (18°F) below 15°C (59°F), the storage life increases by three or four times. Storing in a freezer at -20°C (-4°F) gives typical storage times of 5-10 years for most dried fruits. The quality of defrosted dried fruits should be similar to that

of newly dried fruits.

- Exposure. Store in the dark. Exposure to humidity, light and air during storage adversely affects storage life. Light also fades colour and destroys vitamins A and C.
- Packaging. All packaging materials should be airtight, moisture-proof, insect-proof and rodent-proof. Heat-sealed thick plastic bags or freezer bags should have as much air removed as possible. Vacuum packing, using a domestic-scale machine (see Resources section), is an option. If using jars, fill as full as possible to minimise the amount of air in the jar.

Vacuum packing and refrigerating can each double storage times, while freezing dried fruits can increase storage times by five- or tenfold.

Forest garden fruit loaf

100g (3½oz) mixed dried fruits (e.g. apples, pears, plums, mulberries)

250ml (8¾fl oz) boiling water

30g (1oz) butter

150g (5¼oz) golden caster sugar

100g (3½oz) light muscovado sugar

1 egg, beaten

300g (10½oz) self-raising flour

1 tsp allspice

You will need a 1.5l (2¾ pint) loaf tin.

Preheat the oven to 180°C, (350°F / Gas Mark 4).

Some of the dried fruit may need to be chopped into smaller pieces if it has been dried in long strips – this makes the loaf easier to slice when cooked.

Add the dried fruit to a mixing bowl with the boiling water, butter and sugar, stir together and leave to cool.

Add the egg and allspice and sift in the flour, stirring the ingredients together with a wooden spoon until fully combined and the consistency of a sponge-cake batter. Line the loaf tin with baking parchment, spoon the mixture into it, and place in the centre of the oven. Bake for 1 hour 20 minutes. Check that the loaf is cooked through by pushing a knife into the centre, all the way through. If the knife comes out clean, the loaf is cooked; if it comes out with batter on it, return the loaf to the oven for 15 minutes and test again.

Remove the loaf from the tin immediately and place on a cooling rack. Serve warm, spread with butter, with a nice cup of English tea.

Fruit leathers

A fruit leather is a chewy fruit product, made by puréeing fresh fruit to a smooth thick liquid, which is then poured on to a flat surface and dried. As it dries it takes on a leather-like appearance and texture. When dry it is pulled off the drying surface and still holds its shape.

Fruit leathers are an ideal way of using up slightly bruised, overripe or otherwise blemished fruits which perhaps cannot be processed another way. Leathers can be made from a single fruit or from mixtures, and can also have spices and other ingredients added. With acid fruits, the acidity tends to intensify when dried, so it is best to mix these with a sweeter fruit pulp – plum pulp is a good choice, because it does not have a strong taste that could mask the flavour of other fruits.

General method for fruit leathers

Prepare the fruit as listed in the table on page 38. Purée the fruit until very smooth, adding little or no water if possible, then sieve out any seeds – the latter is done most easily using a Moulinex sieve.

Combine fruits after they have been puréed and add any spices or sweeteners (e.g. sugar, stevia, honey, agave syrup.) You can add other things to the fruit pulp, such as ground nuts or oat flakes, and make a really substantial food product.

Line a drying tray with a fruit-leather sheet: polyester film / plastic sheet (Mylar®), non-stick baking parchment, food-grade plastic or cling film (the latter needs to be taped down). Pour the purée on to the drying tray and spread evenly, aiming for thickness of 4-7mm (1/8-1/4") – the edges dry quicker, so it can be slightly thicker there; thinner in the centre. Leave a border around the purée to allow for spreading during drying.

About 500ml (18fl oz) of purée is needed for a drying tray of 45x35cm (12x14"). Dry at 57°C (135°F), until it feels leather-like and pliable – there should be no sticky spots in the centre – and peels cleanly from the sheet. This takes 16-26 hours in a dehydrator. Remove the leather from the sheet while it is still warm and roll it up into a cylinder, which can then be cut into sections and stored in sealed plastic bags or glass jars. The storage information for fruits, page 32, applies equally to fruit leathers.

Autumn olive & plum leather

This is a favourite in the Crawford household, utilising the great reddish speckled fruits of autumn olive. On their own they are quite tart, so we add in plum pulp (plums considered good for only culinary use are usually fine). We make this in September or October when the autumn olive fruits are ripe, and use either fresh or frozen plums.

Approximate ratios:
This depends on how sweet you want the end product to be. We usually use 3 parts plum to 1 part autumn olive (which corresponds to weight of fruit as well, e.g. 3kg plums to 1kg autumn olive).

Put the autumn olive fruits in a pan with a very small amount of water and bring to the boil. Keep boiling for a few minutes to soften the fruit, then put them through a Moulinex sieve to remove the seeds.

Prepare the plums by de-stoning, then place in a food blender and whizz into a pulp.

Mix the plum and autumn olive pulps together.

Ladle the pulp on to a tray lined with a suitable fruit-leather sheet and dry at around 57°C (135°F) for about 24 hours. Roll up and cut into suitably sized sections before storing in airtight containers.

Blackcurrant & plum leather

This is another Crawford favourite, which preserves the rich blackcurrant flavour of the fruit.

Approximate ratios:
1 part blackcurrant to 3 parts plum.

Purée the ripe blackcurrants. The seeds are tiny and you do not need to de-seed them. Prepare the plums by de-stoning, then place in a food blender and whizz into a pulp.

Mix the pulps together.

Ladle the pulp on to a tray lined with a suitable fruit-leather sheet and dry at around 57°C (135°F) for about 20 hours. Roll up and cut into sections before storing in airtight containers.

The leather shown in the photos below used 500g (1lb 2oz) blackcurrants to 1.7kg (3lb 12oz) plums (which reduced to 1.5kg / 3lb 5oz after de-stoning). The plums were 'Gypsy' cherry plums, which ripen very early, and are freestone, so quick to prepare. This made enough pulp to cover about seven dehydrator trays. Each tray was 38x38cm (approx. 16x16"), so pulp was spread in about a 30x30cm (12x12") square to allow for some spreading.

Blackcurrant and plum fruit leather, using cherry plums. 2012 was a very wet season and some of the plums had split – which is fine. The leather on the sheet shown here took 19 hours to dry. (The actual drying time will depend on air humidity, which depends on the weather!)

Fruit preparation for making fruit leathers			
Fruit	Preparation	Combine with	Spice/flavouring suggestions
Apples	Core, purée with or without skins in a small amount of water or juice. Alternatively, cook and purée.	Any fruits	Allspice, cinnamon, cloves, coriander, lemon, mint, nutmeg, orange, vanilla
Apricots	Remove stone, purée with skins.	Apple, plum	Allspice, cinnamon, cloves, coriander, lemon, nutmeg, orange
Autumn olives	Purée, sieve to remove seeds.	Plum	
Blackberries & hybrid berries	Purée, sieve to remove most of seeds.	Apple	Cinnamon, lemon
Blueberries	Purée whole.	Apple, peach (bland on its own)	Cinnamon, coriander, lemon
Cherries	Remove stones, purée. Heat to almost boiling and cool.	Apple, raspberry, rhubarb	Almond, cinnamon, lemon, orange
Cranberries	Purée	Apple, pear, plum	Cinnamon, cloves, ginger, lemon, orange
Currants	Purée	Plum	
Grapes	Purée, sieve to remove seeds, cook to thicken.	Apple, raspberry	Lemon
Haws	Boil for 5 minutes, sieve to remove seeds.	Plum	
Medlars	Halve, sieve to remove skins & seeds.	Currants	
Peaches & nectarines	Boil for 2 minutes to remove skins. Halve, remove stones, purée.	Apple, blueberry, plum, raspberry	Almond, cinnamon, cloves, ginger, nutmeg
Pears	Peel, core, purée.	Apple, cranberry, rhubarb	Cinnamon, cloves, coriander, lemon, nutmeg, orange
Plum	Remove stones, purée.	Apple, apricot, peach, pear, all acid fruits*	Cinnamon, coriander, lemon, orange
Raspberries	Purée, sieve to remove seeds.	Apple	Lemon, mint, orange
Rhubarb	Steam until tender, purée.	Cherry, plum, raspberry, strawberry	Lemon, orange
Strawberries	Purée, sieve to remove seeds.	Apple, rhubarb, peach	Lemon, orange

* i.e. autumn olives, blackberries, cranberries, currants, haws, raspberries, rhubarb.

Drying nuts

In a climate such as the UK's, nuts in autumn have to be dried to store, otherwise within a week or so they will start to mould. Nuts should ideally be dried within 24 hours of harvesting. If you store nuts too damp, you'll get an unpleasant mouldy surprise a few weeks or months later. Try to harvest your nuts frequently and before major spells of rain. Nuts lying on the ground in rain can absorb a lot of water, which you then need to get rid of by additional drying.

Nuts can be washed in water to remove soil and debris; any nuts that float should be discarded, as they will be empty or bad (note that with some nuts, such as hazels, it is quite normal for a large percentage – up to 25 per cent – to be empty). Nuts, unlike fruits, are normally harvested from the ground, where they can very quickly pick up fungal moulds within a day or two, so washing can be important.

Spread nuts in single layers on drying trays. Unshelled nuts will take 24-48 hours or more to dry, and shelled kernels 8-12 hours or more to dry, at the optimum temperatures listed in the table below. Nuts dried in their shells store for much longer (2-3 years) than nuts dried after shelling (6 months or so). Nuts are also much easier to shell once dried, and the shells are more brittle – so nuts are usually dried in-shell.

These drying times are for British conditions, where nut moisture content at harvest is usually much higher than (say) in California! It is worth doing moisture tests, in the same way as for fruits (see box on page 32), to make sure the nuts are dry enough to store, though it is not as easy to judge dryness in nuts as it is for fruits.

If you have a dry greenhouse or polytunnel – i.e. one with low humidity, so not full of plants – then trays of nuts can be placed inside it to dry. Leave doors open to ensure a decent air flow. As long as the weather is dry and relatively sunny, the nuts should dry within 2-7 days. If the weather is wet, then even here the nuts may not dry without extra heat applied, for example by using a fan heater or greenhouse heater.

After drying, store nuts in airtight plastic, metal or glass containers below 20°C (68°F). Oily nuts (e.g. almonds, hazels, walnuts) should store for 2 or 3 years if well dried, while starchy nuts (e.g. chestnuts) will store for much longer. Dried shelled oily nuts will only store for a few months.

Drying advice for common nuts				
Nut (all in shell)	Water content (by weight)	Preparation	Drying	Dryness test / comments
Almonds	15-20%	None	Dry to 10% moisture or less. Dry shelled almonds to 6%.	For mechanical shelling, dryness to 8-10% moisture is needed.
Black walnuts	25-35%	Wash	Dry to 12% moisture at 25-43°C (77-110°F) – typically takes 30-50 hours.	Weigh
Butternuts	25-35%	Wash	As for black walnuts (above).	Weigh

(Cont.)

Drying advice for common nuts				
Nut (all in shell)	Water content (by weight)	Preparation	Drying	Dryness test / comments
Chestnuts	60%	Wash	Dry to 15% moisture at 40-50°C (104-122°F) – may take 3-5 days. Less than 7% moisture is needed to make good chestnut flour which doesn't cake – may take a further 2-7 days.	Weigh to determine moisture. Dry nuts have brittle shells that break up quite easily. On a small scale, fill a sack half full and beat it on a hard floor or wall, then winnow to clean. 15% moisture is ideal for chestnuts to be eventually rehydrated, and gives storage for over a year.
Hazelnuts	25-35%	Float off empty nuts	Dry at 40-50°C (104-122°F) to achieve 7-8% moisture – typically takes 48 hours.	Weigh
Heartnuts	25-35%	Wash	As for walnuts.	Weigh
Hickories	25-35%	Wash	As for black walnuts.	Weigh
Pecans	25-35%	None	Dry to 12% moisture at 25-43°C (77-110°F) – typically takes 10-20 hours.	Weigh
Walnuts	25-35%	None	Dry to 12% moisture at 25-43°C (77-110°F) – typically takes 20-40 hours. Dry shelled walnuts to 8%.	Membrane between the two walnut shell halves should be crisp and not rubbery.

Drying methods

There are various ways of physically drying foods. Some – notably solar drying – work best in hot, sunny continental climates, while others work anywhere. In the UK, with its typically damp, cloudy conditions, you cannot rely solely on solar drying, so some energy input is going to be required.

Using a dehydrator

The easiest way to dry foods in any climate is to use an electric dehydrator. These are purpose-built machines, easy to use and with a reasonable guarantee of success.

A good-quality dehydrator will yield a better-quality, more nutritious dried product than any other method of drying. It allows for drying overnight or any other time period, and requires minimal time for watching, turning or rotating the food. Three important features that are desirable in a dehydrator are:

- An adjustable thermostat – allows for different temperatures for different products.
- Fan-blown air circulation – removes moisture and reduces drying times.
- An efficient heat source – large enough for the drying area and more efficient if controlled by thermostat.

One more feature which is very useful, though not essential, is a built-in timer (you can also use a separate plug-in timer if preferred). A timer allows you to set the dryer going for a specified period of time, so if you forget to check it at exactly the right moment, the food will not be over-dried.

Circular dehydrators usually have the heating unit in the base and may rely on convection to supply the airflow, in which case they will be slow. They require you to rotate the trays, as the lower trays dry first. The drying trays will have holes in the centre, which reduces the usable drying area.

Dehydrators with a fan and heater at one side and a horizontal airflow over drying trays provide more even drying, do not require tray rotation, have more drying area for the same volume and are more versatile. They are more expensive, though. A personal favourite is the American Excalibur range, which is excellent.

Power consumption by dehydrators varies with the model, the drying temperature and weather conditions – more power is needed in high humidity and colder conditions. Martin's 9-tray Excalibur model uses about 400W when drying at 57°C (135°F) in late autumn, about 30W of which is used by the air circulation fan and the rest by the heater element.

Stove-top drying

Those with an Aga or Rayburn-type stove, which is on constantly, can utilise the heat for drying. A metal rack can be placed on the stove top, or a slatted tray attached to the wall higher above the stove. However, the temperature is difficult to control with this method, and air circulation is variable. Constant heat is required until the food is dried, and the dried product is rarely as good-quality (less flavoursome and more likely to have mould taints) as if dried using a dehydrator. The bottom oven of these stoves can also be used, but the door usually needs to be left ajar to allow for some air circulation.

Oven drying

Oven drying (in a conventional oven) can take two or three times longer than drying in a dehydrator – making it less energy-efficient and more costly – and time is required to tend and rotate the food. Food dried in an oven is usually darker, more brittle and less flavoursome than food dried in a dehydrator. The temperatures are often higher than in a dehydrator, which leads to nutrient losses from the food. Fruits with a very high moisture content, or those which thick skins (e.g. plums), are very difficult to oven-dry due to the likelihood of the surfaces case-hardening in the higher temperatures.

Test the oven temperature with a thermometer before using it to dry. Most oven temperature scales do not even start at the temperatures you want to dry at (50-60°C/122-140°F), so you need to prop the oven door open to achieve a temperature in this range. Convection or fan ovens are best, as these create an airflow. For greater air circulation, use fine-mesh drying trays or oven racks covered with nylon netting or cheesecloth to lay on the slices of fruit or the nuts.

Solar drying

In areas with hot, dry, sunny summers and autumns, solar drying is an option. Ideally, outside temperatures of 30°C (86°F) are required for this to work well.

It may seem obvious, but you need full sun for a solar dehydrator to work. A warm but cloudy day is next to useless. Not only do you need sun, but you often need sun for more than one day in succession, and of course you get no drying at night-time, so for fruits (or nuts with a high water content, i.e. chestnuts) they need to be sufficiently dried on the first day so that spoilage is slowed enough during the night-time lull. The dryer needs to be sited where it is unobscured by trees or buildings, so it can receive maximum light.

In many types of solar dryer, the fruit is laid out on trays in the sun, which results in some loss of nutrients (although the sun's ultraviolet rays also have a sterilising effect, which slows the growth of some microorganisms). It is better, if possible, to make some kind of solar collector that heats air which is then passed through a drying chamber in the dark.

There are no commercial solar dryer around, so if you want one you'll have to make your own. There are plenty of designs available online (most of the users, you'll see, come from very sunny places!). Remember that the insides of dryers need to be cleanable – so wood is not so practical (it also warps a lot with the moisture-laden air of drying fruit).

Because solar dryer can take several days to dry moisture-rich fruits, such foods must have a fairly high sugar and acid content to prevent spoilage during the drying process.

Nevertheless, solar-dried foods tend to have lower quality and nutritional value than foods dried under controlled conditions, simply because of the fluctuating natural conditions. As much as 50 per cent of the nutritive value can be lost.

The fruits most suitable for solar drying are those with higher sugar levels: apples, grapes, plums, apricots, nectarines, cherries, peaches, figs, pears.

Combination systems

Solar dryers can be made more versatile by combining some elements of artificial dryers with the solar function. Adding a fan to increase the airflow can be very effective – and solar-powered fans are available. Adding a thermostat-controlled heating element would extend the potential further, reducing drying times and compensating for cooler night-time temperatures and periods of dull weather.

You can link up a home-made solar air heater with an electric dehydrator quite easily. Dehydrators such as the Excalibur draw air in though the back of the unit, and this can be connected to draw the air from a solar air heating panel. On a bright sunny day in the UK it is quite possible to achieve air temperatures of 50-60°C (122-140°F) from solar heating panels, which is quite hot enough to dry fruits and fruit leathers, though too hot for drying nuts. When the air is this hot, the thermostat inside the dehydrator will not switch the heating element on, so the only power used will be that for the fan in the unit. As soon as the weather turns cloudy, the solar heating panel will

Martin's home-built nut dryer. The stack of trays can be pulled out on wheels for inspection.

be of little use, but the heating element will then cut in.

There is also potential for using a wood-burning system to heat air that is circulated around trays of drying food. You'll have to build your own system, but for budding engineers with plenty of firewood this could be an interesting option.

Larger-scale drying of fruits and nuts

Most larger-scale processors end up building their own dryers. The important factors, again, are air circulation and warm air. Unheated dry air can be used, but increases the drying time by a factor of five to seven. The moist warm air that is emitted by the dryer can be passed across a heat exchanger to reclaim some of the heat from the air, or the air can be recirculated, thereby reducing running costs.

For drying nuts, in general an airflow of 15-30 cubic metres per minute per cubic metre of nuts (15-30 cubic feet per minute per cubic foot of nuts) is required. Our home-built nut drier for walnuts, pictured opposite, was built around the dimensions of standard food-grade plastic trays (40x60cm/1'4"x2') and can fit 20 such trays in at a time, which is a lot of nuts (about 60kg/132lb).

Commercial control systems have been designed that signal a stop to the drying process on the basis of the temperature difference of the air fed to the nuts and the air leaving the nuts. This temperature difference reduces as the nuts get drier. When the air leaving is only 3-4°C (5-7°F) cooler than the inlet air, the batch is dry. The exact difference needed varies with the nut layer depth and volume, the airflow and the initial nut moisture level.

CHAPTER 4

Fermenting

Fermentation is a natural process in which foods are broken down over time by microorganisms and are thereby chemically altered. There are different kinds of fermentation involving different types of food, microorganisms and conditions, and humans have been experimenting with these for millennia. When certain microorganisms are present and are given the ideal conditions in which to work, they will make the food 'environment' uninhabitable for other, harmful microorganisms, thus preserving the food. These 'helpful' microorganisms come in the form of particular genera of bacteria and yeasts that are present naturally on the food itself or in the air. Food preservation has probably been the main motivation for fermenting foods, but the art has evolved through the desire to create particular flavours and textures that we have come to love.

Possibly the first type of fermentation harnessed by people was in the creation of alcohol, the earliest evidence of which, found in the Middle East, dates back seven thousand years. Alcohol is created by a natural yeast which, under anaerobic (without oxygen) conditions, converts fruit and vegetable sugars into ethyl alcohol and carbon dioxide. One of the simplest alcoholic drinks is cider: apple juice will become cider in the space of a week if the weather is warm, and if left longer and exposed to the air it will become vinegar, as airborne yeasts and bacteria move in to devour the remaining sugars. This is why airlocks are used when making alcohol – to keep the aerobic microorganisms out so that the anaerobic yeasts can dominate.

Fermentation is also the process involved in making leavened bread. Here, too, yeast is the active ingredient: it consumes sugars in the grain and releases carbon dioxide. Kneading activates the gluten in the flour, and small bubbles of carbon dioxide become trapped in the glutinous dough, causing it to rise. Historically, people began leavening bread with only the yeast that occurred naturally on the grain itself, which was activated when water was added to the flour, creating what we now call sourdough.

A genus of bacteria called *Lactobacillus* can occur naturally in milk, fruit and vegetables, and creates lactic acid which, like alcohol and vinegar, acts as a preservative by creating a hostile environment for other microorganisms. When *Lactobacillus* is at work the process is known as 'lacto fermentation'. It is believed that this bacterium was first harnessed to create yogurt and cheese from milk, and this association with dairy products has led to the misconception that 'lacto' refers to the lactose present in cows' milk. In fact, *Lactobacillus* is also responsible for many vegetable ferments, including sauerkrauts and pickles.

In the past, when people were not aware of the different strains of bacteria and yeast at work on their food, fermentation was a simple activity where nature was given a helping hand and then left to its own devices. Today, science has discovered which microorganisms are responsible for different kinds of fermentation, and how to control them. These natural processes have been refined to such a degree that nothing is left to chance. It is now possible to buy specific cultures for making your own beer, wine, bread, yogurt and cheese, for example, and an array of specialist equipment is available. All this can give the impression that fermentation is very complex and scientific, requiring a well-equipped laboratory, but this is simply not the case. So long as we encourage the 'good bacteria' and not the 'bad' ones, we have nothing to fear!

The term 'wild fermentation' describes the practice of fermenting foods using only microorganisms which occur naturally on the food itself, in the water added, or in the surrounding air. The methods described in this chapter are basic wild fermentation techniques that anyone can try without the need for specialist equipment. There is no shortage of reading material on more specialist and refined methods for the enthusiastic brewer, baker or pickler – see the Resources section for a couple of examples.

Beyond the preserving qualities and flavour experiences, there are also numerous health benefits of fermentation. The microorganisms in these foods are our internal allies, working away within our intestines. The human digestive system is home to around 400 different species of bacteria, known collectively as our intestinal flora. This internal ecosystem benefits from diversity and, when in balance, enables efficient digestion of food and effective absorption of the nutrients within it. 'Good' bacteria, such as the *Lactobacillus* genus, help to break down foods that we would otherwise struggle to digest, such as starches and complex proteins, converting them to valuable nutrients such as glucose and amino acids. This enables more of the food to be converted to energy, and for excess calories to be stored as fat – essential for our survival. The bacteria also make certain minerals 'bio-available', meaning that, as a result of digestion by the bacteria, they can be absorbed by us. Some bacteria actually create certain nutrients as by-products of their own metabolic processes, including vitamin K, B vitamins and omega-3 fatty acids.

Our intestinal flora can also help to break down carcinogens and toxins and help the walls of the digestive tract regenerate and stay healthy. For this reason, fermented foods are used in holistic and complementary medicine to reputedly combat cancer and other diseases. A healthy intestinal environment boosts the body's immune system, and the regular introduction of good bacteria through fermented foods can lead to better heath. It is important, then, to make a distinction between 'live' fermented foods and those which have been subject to processing, for example pasteurisation, that has killed the microorganisms which made the product. Many pickles, yogurts and cheeses have been pasteurised in order to comply with hygiene requirements in mass production and therefore have none of the health benefits just described. It is possible to buy unpasteurised products – just check the label – or, better still, make them yourself!

Harnessing microorganisms, whether to make bread rise, beer fizz or vegetables keep, is not simply about preservation or health benefits, it is also about flavour, texture and aroma. For example, salt has been used traditionally in many cultures to preserve dried or smoked foods, but in fermented foods it is combined with water and subjected to a process by which the microorganisms can transform it into something completely different. Vinegar, itself a product of fermentation, can also be used (whether live or pasteurised) as a preserving medium without further fermentation – as described in Chapter 2 – since, as with salt, most microorganisms cannot live in it. The decision to make fermented foods is largely driven by taste and the pleasure of experimentation.

A common cause for hesitation with home fermentation is the fear of food poisoning. However, if something has gone wrong with the process your nose will soon inform you – it will smell bad and taste bad, and is unlikely to make it as far as your stomach! Wild fermentation is not fail-safe, and trial and error is the key to success, but on the whole it is incredibly simple and reliable as long as you follow the basic rules.

Vegetable ferments

It is likely that any vegetable you can think of has been preserved using fermentation somewhere, at some time. There are various different techniques, including salting and brining, which are described here, but they all have one thing in common – simplicity. You will need some very basic equipment (see right) and suitably sized jars for storage. While the food is fermenting, it should be placed in a part of the house at normal room temperature (see 'Salting ratios' box, page 48) and where the temperature is not too variable.

The basics: a ceramic crock, salt and storage jars.

Equipment

You will need a plastic, glass or ceramic container such as a traditional fermentation crock in which to ferment your foods. If using plastic, ensure it is 'food grade' – one option is to reuse the sort of buckets that contain foods such as mayonnaise or tahini in bulk. Do not use metal containers, as they can corrode in brine and vinegar. It helps if the container is cylindrical with straight sides, as that makes it easier to weigh down the contents. For this you will need a ceramic plate that fits snugly into your container to push the vegetables below the liquid, thus keeping them free from surface mould, and some kind of weight to hold it down. People use all sorts of things for this, from rocks to jars filled with water. The important thing is that your container, plate and weight have been sterilised (see box, right). You will also need a cloth, such as a tea towel or piece of muslin or cheesecloth, and string to tie it on with. This will keep insects out but let the microorganisms in.

Salting

The simplest of all fermentation techniques, this is the traditional method used to create sauerkraut.

Sterilising, bottling and storage of ferments

To sterilise weights and metal lids, place in a saucepan, submerge in water and boil for 5 minutes. To sterilise glass jars and bottles, place in an oven at 100°C (212°F / Gas Mark ¼) for 20 minutes. For plastic and ceramic containers, wash thoroughly and rinse with boiling water (it's not usually practical, owing to their size and/or material, to boil such containers; also, because they are usually used for making ferments rather than storing them, sterilising is often less critical).

When your cultured creations have reached perfection they must be sealed from the air in order to halt the fermentation process. If using jars with metal lids, use a layer of plastic – cut-up pieces of carrier bag work well – to form a barrier between the liquid and the metal, as ferments can corrode metal over time. It helps to fill jars to the brim in order to exclude as much air as possible, to reduce the formation of mould on the surface. Storing in the fridge will also help with this, although some surface mould may still form. If it does, it can simply be skimmed off with a spoon.

Once decanted and sealed, remember to label the containers clearly with the contents and date. It is hard to give a fixed shelf life to living foods – most will store for several months – but recording the date can help you to decide which jars should be consumed first.

It can also be used with grated root vegetables to create sour slaws. Adding salt to the dry vegetables draws out the liquid within them via osmosis, creating a flavoursome brine in which they are fermented.

Salting ratios

3 tbsp salt : 2kg (4lb 6oz) vegetables
For brine solution:
1 tbsp salt : 250ml (8¾fl oz) water

The above ratios are approximate and flexible. The exact conditions in your kitchen will be unique, and will also vary through the year. The warmer the temperature, the faster things will ferment. If the conditions are very warm, you can increase the amount of salt used, to help prevent the food from souring too quickly or going bad. Conversely, in a cold environment you can use a little less salt in order to speed things up. Your taste is also an important factor: generally, the longer you ferment something, the more sour it becomes, so if you like milder, sweeter flavours you will need to check the brine more regularly in order to prevent it from becoming too sour.

This technique can be applied to many different kinds of vegetable and will have a different effect, depending on how much water and natural sugars the vegetable contains. Sometimes the vegetables will need a little brine added to them, especially when using thinner leaf vegetables, as they don't contain much water themselves. The basic method is to sprinkle salt over layers of shredded or grated vegetables, then compress the vegetables in a container for at least a week, possibly with a little brine added to help it along, depending on how much liquid the salt draws out from the vegetables.

It pays to use good-quality sea salt rather than processed table salt. Sea salt contains trace minerals from the sea or lake from which it was taken. It is more natural, and has a better flavour and higher nutritional value. Table salt usually comes from mines, is heavily processed and contains additives such as anti-clumping agents.

Sauerkraut

This simple recipe, traditionally made with cabbage, can also be made with perennial brassica leaves such as 'Nine Star' broccoli and 'Daubenton' kale. Make sure you pick leaves when they are really fresh and succulent, and remember that they will shrink down as they ferment, so pick plenty.

Brassica or other leaves, shredded
Additional herbs and vegetables of your choice (e.g. onion, garlic, dill, fennel), shredded or grated
Sea salt (see box, left, for quantities)

You will need a suitable large container, a plate, a weight and a cloth.

The leaves should make up the bulk of the mix: around 4 parts leaves to 1 part other vegetables and herbs, but you can experiment with what you have available and according to taste. Mix the shredded leaves and vegetables and spread them, a handful at a time, over the base of your container. Sprinkle some salt after every few handfuls, aiming to distribute it evenly between layers of vegetables.

48

When all the vegetables are in the container, cover them with the plate and push it down firmly, compressing them as much as possible. Put the weight on top of the plate and cover the container with the cloth. Tie the cloth around with string to secure it over the container – this will keep insects out but let the micro-organisms in.

Over the next day or two, press down on the weight occasionally to encourage the process, and after 24-48 hours enough liquid should have been drawn out of the vegetables to cover the plate. If after 48 hours the plate is not covered with brine, add a little brine solution to ensure the vegetables are submerged. Give the sauerkraut a gentle stir and then replace the plate.

Check the container daily and remove any mould that forms on the surface of the liquid using a spoon. After 1 week, taste the brine daily until you are satisfied with the flavour.

Transfer the sauerkraut to sterilised storage jars, label them with the date and contents and store in the fridge. It will keep for at least 3 months when refrigerated.

Try using this method to make a sour slaw with grated root vegetables, garlic and herbs. You can also create a Korean-style kimchi with mixed forest garden vegetables, Szechuan pepper and elephant garlic.

Brining (pickling)

Brining is an all-inclusive method of fermentation, applicable to pretty much any kind of fruit or vegetable. Essentially, you create a brine solution, submerge your chosen food in it and wait. Some recipes, such as brined garlic or capers, are very simple and use only one food ingredient. Others, such as some traditional Indian pickles, are more exotic and complex.

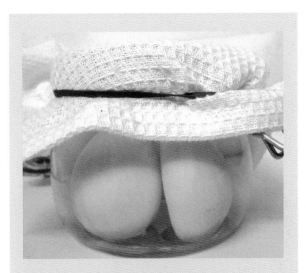

Brined elephant garlic

1 elephant garlic bulb, separated and peeled
2 tbsp sea salt
400ml (14fl oz) water

You will need a 0.5l (18fl oz) sterilised glass storage jar and a piece of cloth.

Add the salt to the water and stir until fully dissolved. Place the peeled cloves of garlic into the storage jar and pour in the brine solution. The cloves are so big that you can wedge them in against each other and prevent them from floating to the top. Make sure there is at least 2cm (¾") of brine above the garlic cloves, and fix the cloth to the rim of the jar with an elastic band or string.

Allow to ferment for approximately 1 week, tasting the brine daily and removing any mould that forms on the surface. When the garlic is to your liking, if you have had a lot of mould you may choose to empty the jar contents into a clean bowl, re-sterilise the jar and return the contents to it for storage. Label and date the jar and store in a cool place. It will keep for several months out of the fridge, but refrigeration helps to reduce surface mould.

This same method can be used to preserve the peppery seed pods of nasturtiums to make nasturtium 'capers'.

You will need a suitable container with a capacity of at least 2l (70fl oz / 3¼ pints), a plate, a weight and a cloth.

In a large jug, combine the salt and water and stir until the salt has fully dissolved.

Place the whole garlic cloves, peppercorns, fennel and apple mint in the bottom of your container. Add the snowbell tree fruits on top, and pour over the brine. Place the plate on top of the ingredients and push down so that the brine covers the surface of the plate. Sit the weight on top to hold the plate under the liquid. Cover the container with the cloth and tie it around with string.

Check the container daily for mould on the surface of the brine, which can be taken off with a spoon. Taste the pickles after a week to see how they are progressing: they will take 1-4 weeks to fully sour, depending on the temperature of the room and how sour you like them. Once in jars, they will keep for several months out of the fridge, but refrigeration helps to reduce surface mould.

Snowbell pickles

Makes approximately 4 x 400ml (14fl oz) jars

500g (1lb 2oz) snowbell tree fruits, washed and trimmed

1l (35fl oz / 1¾ pints) water, at room temperature

50g (1¾oz) coarse sea salt

3 garlic cloves

1 tsp whole black peppercorns

A few fennel leaves and flowerheads

Sprig of fresh apple mint

Fruit ferments

The most common and popular way of fermenting fruit is to create alcohol and vinegar. As indicated at the beginning of this chapter, alcohol can be created by simply adding fruit to water, sealing it from the air and waiting. Exposing the alcohol to the air and waiting a little longer will create vinegar. The basic method, then, is simple, but honing it to create a delicious alcoholic tipple takes time, experimentation and passion for the finished product. There is plenty of literature available on the subject of home brewing, so here we focus on making vinegars. Simple liqueurs (alcohol infusions) are described in Chapter 2.

Fruit vinegars

Towards the end of the harvest period in late autumn you may find yourself with an abundance of fruit to process. This may leave you with peelings, stones and cores, or an excess that is rapidly spoiling. Fruit vinegar is a great way to use up scraps and surplus, and can in turn be used to preserve other excess from the garden (see Chapter 2). The recipe below is made with plums, but you can use the same ratios with any fruit.

Plum vinegar

Makes approximately 4 x 400ml (14fl oz) jars

200g (7oz) plums (or other whole fruit, peelings or cores)
1l (35fl oz / 1¾ pints) water
50g (1¾ oz) granulated sugar

You will need a 1.5l (55fl oz / 2¾ pint) glass storage jar and a piece of cloth.

If using whole fruit, start by chopping the fruit into chunks. Add the fruit to the bottom of the jar.

Add the sugar to the water and stir until the granules have dissolved. Add this solution to the jar and cover the top with the cloth, held in place with an elastic band or string.

After a few days the liquid will become darker as the fruit infuses into the water. Now strain out the fruit and return the liquid to the jar. It will take a further 2-3 weeks to fully sour, so keep checking it and stir it occasionally. You will be able to smell when it is ready, but taste it too, to judge when the flavour is right. Transfer to bottles and label with the contents and date. Fruit vinegars don't need to be refrigerated, as they don't contain any solid organic content.

Cider and wine vinegars

If you grow apples, you may find that at times you have more than you can handle – there is only so much crumble one can eat! Juicing is a great way to get through fruit before it spoils, and an easy way to get fruit into children's diets. However, fresh juice has a shorter refrigerator life than pasteurised juice, and sometimes it start to turn before you get to the bottom of the bottle.

One easy solution to this is to save the 'dregs' of juice bottles and allow them to ferment into cider. The juice must be kept in a sealed, sterilised container and left somewhere warm and dark for about a week. Check the container daily and let out the carbon dioxide gas that builds up. After a week, transfer the cider to a glass storage jar or bowl, cover with a cloth and leave it in a warm place for another 2 weeks, checking and stirring occasionally. When your cider vinegar is ready you can bottle it in sterilised bottles and it will keep for months. Many people hail apple cider vinegar as a health tonic and drink it daily to aid digestion. It is also very useful for cooking and can be used for pickling, infusions and salad dressings.

Wine vinegar can be made in the same way, and can be created from wines of all varieties.

PART 2

RECIPES USING FRESH PRODUCE

Plants included in these chapters

CHAPTER 5

Spring

Alexanders (*Smyrnium olusatrum*)

Also known as black lovage

Brought to Britain by the Romans, alexanders has been naturalised since then, especially near the coast. It is a biennial, sending up vertical stems in its second year with typical umbellifer-type flowers followed by heads of black seeds.

The entire plant can be used for food, and all parts are high in minerals and vitamin C. The leaves and young stems are harvested mainly in late winter and spring, when fresh and glossy, and are at their best before the plant has grown very tall. They make a delicious spring treat, with a strong flavour somewhat resembling lovage and celery. The stems are crisp and sweet and can be eaten like asparagus, while the leaves can be used like a herb in salads, stew and soups.

The ripe seeds can be harvested in summer and stored dry. When ground they are highly aromatic (with the same flavour as the leaves) and used as a seasoning. They were formerly preserved in wine, and the liquid drunk to prevent scurvy.

The 1-year-old roots are also edible. These are thick and fleshy, strongly flavoured like the rest of the plant, and are eaten cooked. They can be lifted all through the winter.

Alexanders & Babington's leek linguine

Serves 4

100g (3½oz) alexanders stems, chopped into 3cm (1⅛") lengths

50g (1¾oz) alexanders leaves, roughly chopped

150g (5¼oz) Babington's leeks

120g (4¼oz) oyster mushrooms, sliced lengthways

30g (1oz) butter

400g (14oz) linguine

300ml (10½fl oz) crème fraîche

1 tbsp chopped fresh parsley

1 tbsp chopped fresh dill

Remove the soft bulb and tough green leaves of the Babington's leeks and slice the white stems into 1cm (⅜") rounds. Melt the butter in a deep frying pan and add the stems, leeks and mushrooms. Gently sauté for 8 minutes or until soft and golden.

Add the linguine to a pan of boiling water and cook according to the instructions on the packet. Strain the pasta and return to the saucepan. Immediately stir in the alexanders leaves, allowing the hot pasta to wilt them. Add the remaining vegetables, crème fraîche and herbs to the linguine and gently mix together until the crème fraîche is covering all the ingredients.

Serve immediately on to warmed plates or bowls.

Spicy alexanders & tomato soup

Serves 4

50g (1¾oz) alexanders leaves, roughly chopped

2 Babington's leeks, finely chopped

1 tbsp olive oil

1 large onion, finely chopped

1 tsp ground cumin

3 tsp paprika

½ tsp allspice

½ tsp chilli

3 tsp soft brown sugar

2 400g (14oz) tins of tomatoes

800ml (28fl oz) vegetable stock

Preheat the olive oil in a large saucepan. Fry the onion and leeks in the oil over a medium heat for about 5 minutes until they begin to soften. Add the spices and fry for another 2 minutes, then add the sugar and fry for 1 minute. Add more olive oil if necessary to prevent the spices from burning and sticking.

Mash or blend the tinned tomatoes and add them to the saucepan along with the stock and bring to the boil. Add half of the alexanders leaves to the pan, cover and simmer on a low heat for 20 minutes, then add the remaining leaves and simmer for a further 2 minutes.

Serve hot with a chunk of bread drizzled with olive oil and sprinkled with a little salt.

Alexanders stems with bacon

These parcels are great as a starter or a special snack. You will need 4 or 5 stems of pencil thickness per bundle, and 1 or 2 bundles per person.

Alexanders stems and leaves, cut into 10cm (4")
lengths
Salt
Thinly sliced smoked back bacon
Butter
Crème fraîche

Pour about 5cm (2") water into a large saucepan and bring to the boil. Add some salt and then drop in your stems and simmer for 3 minutes. Remove the stems (keeping the water) and place them on to some kitchen paper to dry and cool a little. Separate a rasher of bacon and lay it on to a board, then take 4 or 5 stems and place on one end. Roll the stems up in the rasher firmly and place to one side. Repeat this with the rest of the stems. Melt a knob of butter in a frying pan and lightly fry the bundles, gently turning until the bacon is slightly crisped.

Take a handful of alexanders leaves for every 2 bundles you are making. Remove any bad leaves and thick stalks. Bring the water in the saucepan back to the boil, add the leaves and simmer for about 2 minutes until the leaves have wilted. Remove from the pan with tongs and place on to kitchen paper. Arrange the wilted leaves on a plate and put a generous teaspoon of crème fraîche into the centre, then place a bundle on top. Serve immediately.

Alexanders leaves and stems are great for flavouring soups, stews and other cooked recipes, as well as chopped finely in salads.

Try the stems as a side vegetable: simmer for 3 or 4 minutes and then roll in butter with salt and pepper. If the stems are thick they may be a bit stringy, in which case peel them as you would rhubarb or celery: just run a knife down the sides to remove the threads.

Apple mint (*Mentha suaveolens*)

Apple mint is a favourite general-purpose mint for use in bulk quantities. The leaves and young stems can be used over a very long season – all year round in very mild locations. The leaves are slightly woolly but this does not detract when they are chopped in recipes. Fresh mints are delicious with tomatoes, either cooked in sauces and soups or raw in salads. The refreshing zingy combination is particularly appealing in the summer months, and the simple chilled Spanish soup gazpacho is the perfect way to make use of abundant apple mint crops. Only the more pungent mints – for example, peppermint – are worth drying to store. The milder mints, such as apple mint, lose too much flavour when dried, so either use fresh or preserve them some other way, e.g. in oil or vinegar.

Mints are high in vitamins A and C, calcium, iron, phosphorus and zinc.

Like all mints, apple mint is a spreading plant and should be planted with that in mind. It is fairly shade-tolerant and makes a good underplanting beneath a thin tree or shrub canopy.

To harvest, pinch off the top 5-10cm (2-4") of soft stem and leaves; you can also strip any decent-looking leaves from further down the stems. Plants will put out new side shoots a few weeks later, which can themselves be harvested after a while.

Gazpacho soup with apple mint

Serves 4

3 tbsp finely chopped fresh apple mint

2 400g (14oz) tins of chopped plum tomatoes

1 medium onion, coarsely chopped

2 garlic cloves, crushed

1 red pepper, coarsely chopped

200ml (7fl oz) water

3 tbsp olive oil

1 tbsp balsamic vinegar

1 tsp caster sugar

Salt and ground black pepper

100g (3½oz) cucumber, very finely chopped

2 tbsp chopped fresh coriander leaf

Garnish:

Apple mint leaves

Food processor

Place the tomatoes, onion, garlic and red pepper into a food processor and blend until minced. Add the water, oil, vinegar, sugar, salt and pepper and stir well.

Transfer to a bowl and refrigerate for 30 minutes, or until ready to serve. Before serving stir in the cucumber and herbs and garnish with a twist of black pepper and a couple of apple mint leaves.

Apple mint makes a refreshing tea when the torn leaves are infused in hot water, and when used with fennel leaf is a good digestive tonic after a large meal. This combination also works well in a vinegar infusion to use in salad dressings.

Fresh apple mint is a great addition to a summer herb salad, being soft and mild yet flavoursome, and is good in courgette or squash soups, adding a sweet but earthy tone.

Other recipes using apple mint: Spring forest salad (page 70); Wineberry & apple mint sorbet (page 173); infused vinegars (Part 1, page 26).

Bamboos (*Phyllostachys spp.,*
Pleioblastus simonii, Pseudosasa japonica,
Semiarundinaria fastuosa and *Yushania spp.*)

Bamboo shoots are a hugely popular vegetable in many parts of the world. The new shoots emerge mainly between April and July in temperate climates. To be worth eating, they need to be at least 1cm (⅜") in diameter, so the dwarf bamboos are of little value. Bamboo shoots are high in fibre, protein and minerals – especially iron, zinc, potassium, phosphorus, copper and manganese; also in vitamins B6, C, Niacin and Riboflavin.

Most species are bitter when raw, although a few can be used raw in salads. To remove the bitterness, chop shoots into pieces and steam for 5-10 minutes. Cut shoots will store in a fridge for 3-4 days. To prepare the shoots, the outer leaves have to be stripped off – see 'shredded bamboo method', page 64, for how to do this. Only about the top 30cm (1') is usable from longer shoots.

New shoots grow very fast – up to 25cm (10") per day in the UK – and to be edible they must be harvested before they are more than 80-100cm (2'8"-3'3") high.

Bamboo with beef

Serves 4

200g (7oz) bamboo, prepared and cut into 5-10cm (2-4") lengths

Marinade:

2 tbsp soy sauce

1 tbsp saki, rice or wine vinegar

2 tbsp honey

500g (1lb 2oz) beef steak

2 medium carrots

1 large red pepper

1 large brown onion

250g (9oz) savoy cabbage (or other seasonal green)

180g (6½oz) chestnut mushrooms

A little sesame or vegetable oil

Sauce:

3 crushed garlic cloves

1 tbsp grated ginger

2 tbsp soy sauce

3 tbsp sweet chilli sauce

300ml (10½fl oz) beef stock

Strip off the outer leaves of the bamboo shoots as described overleaf. Boil or steam them for about 5 minutes until the thickest pieces have softened slightly. Strain and put to one side.

Mix together the marinade ingredients in a bowl, adding about 2 tablespoons of boiling water, and stir until the honey has dissolved. Take the beef steak and remove the fat using a sharp knife. Cut the meat into thin strips, around 1cm (⅜") thick and 6-8cm (2½-3") long. Put the strips into the marinade, stir to cover, and put aside while preparing the vegetables.

Cut the carrots, pepper, onion, cabbage and mushrooms into long, thin strips. In a jug, mix together the ingredients for the sauce. Heat a little sesame or vegetable oil in a large wok and run it around the sides. Add the vegetables to the wok and pour over the sauce. Stir-fry for 5 minutes.

While the vegetables are cooking take a second, smaller wok or frying pan and heat a little oil. Using tongs or a slotted spoon transfer the beef strips to the frying pan, then add the bamboo. Stir-fry together on a high heat for 2-3 minutes until the beef is seared on all sides but tender in the middle. If you cook the beef for too long it will be tough and chewy.

Serve the vegetables on a bed of rice or noodles and place the bamboo and beef on top while sizzling hot.

Cooked bamboo shoots can also be eaten as a vegetable on their own. The delicate flavour is reminiscent of peas, runner beans and courgette, and is popular with children who don't like strong flavours. They are delicious with just butter, salt and pepper or in a white sauce with fresh parsley.

Bamboo shoot yum

This salad recipe is based on a traditional north-eastern Thai dish called 'Soop naw mai'. In Thailand bamboo shoots can be bought in jars or tins, pre-cut into thin strips, which gives them the appearance of flat noodles. This can be achieved with fresh bamboo too, as detailed below, and gives the salad a great texture. Thai salads are traditionally pretty hot, as anyone who has sampled the popular green mango salad will know, but you can decide how hot you make it. Using ground, mild chilli powder instead of fresh or dried chilli can help you to regulate the heat so you don't get a nasty surprise with the first mouthful.

Shredded bamboo method

First, strip off the outer leaves. Because they overlap, this needs to be done in two or three sections. Slice the bamboo shoots lengthways from butt to tip. Peel off the outer layer of brown, papery leaves to reveal the first section of bright green and white flesh. Chop off this section and then peel off the next layer of outer leaves, to reveal the next green/white section, and repeat all the way to the tip. You may need to discard about 5cm (2") of the tip as it can be a little dry and papery. Discard the dry brown outer leaves.

Take the bamboo sections and cut them again lengthways so you have quarter sections of shoot. If the shoot is more than 1.5cm (⅝") in diameter, slice it again into eighths. You will see that the shoot is made up of many layers of white flesh which increase in number towards the tip. At the butt you have the thicker, harder inner core with a hollow cavity, divided into hollow cells – a distinctive and familiar character of bamboo. All of this is edible, and for this recipe we want to separate the thin layers of flesh to create noodle-like strips. Pull the layers off the hard core and put to one side. Slice any thicker pieces of core as thinly as possible and put them with the 'noodles'. Taste a piece of the core to see how bitter or starchy it is. The smaller, younger shoots are often delicious eaten raw and do not need cooking. However, the thicker, older shoots can be a little hard and bitter, or starchy, so will need to be boiled or steamed for approximately 5 minutes. For the recipe given here the shoots can be raw or cooked.

Serves 4

150g (5¼oz) prepared shredded bamboo

2 tbsp sweet cicely seeds, finely chopped

4 spring onions

Half a lime, juice and finely grated zest

1 tbsp fish sauce

1 tbsp sesame oil

½ tsp finely chopped fresh or dried red chilli

50g (1¾oz) raw peanuts

Food processor

Prepare the bamboo as described opposite, and if you have cooked it, rinse with cold water, strain and allow to cool. Peel, top and tail the spring onions and slice lengthways into thin strips of about 8cm (3") long. Place the sweet cicely seeds into a large salad bowl with the spring onions. Add the lime juice and zest to the bowl. Add the fish sauce, sesame oil, chilli and bamboo to the bowl and toss together well.

Place the raw peanuts on to a flat baking tray or grill pan and place under a medium grill for 3-5 minutes, watching all the time, until they begin to brown very slightly. Remove and blend in a food processor until they are half ground and cut into small chunks.

Sprinkle the peanuts over the top of the salad and serve.

Beech (*Fagus sylvatica*)

The leaves of various trees and shrubs, including the humble beech tree, make good eating. It isn't really so strange to eat leaves from trees: in the past, when we were all hunter-foragers, they would have provided a regular source of nutrition.

The soft, bright-green leaves of beech are tender with a lemony flavour. They are nice in salads or cooked dishes (added late in the recipe). They do not store for long after being picked but can be preserved in oil, made into pesto, etc.

Nutritionally, beech leaves are likely to be rich in minerals.

Beech trees can become very large in time, but it is easy to cultivate them as bushes in a garden. They do not coppice well but are very tolerant of trimming, so simply give them an overall trim once a year – in late spring or early summer after the harvest season – to keep them at whatever size you want. This makes harvesting much easier, too.

Beech leaves are harvested in mid-spring, from the moment they emerge from the long pointed buds for about 3 weeks until they get too tough.

Recipes using beech: Spring forest salad (page 70); Beech gin liqueur (Part 1, page 27).

Chinese cedar (*Toona sinensis*)

Also known as toon

This Chinese tree (not a cedar as the name suggests, but a deciduous tree) is virtually unknown as an edible in the UK, and is only rarely grown as an ornamental. In China, however, it is widely cultivated as a vegetable and is also used like a herb.

The leaves are compound, on long leaf stalks, with leaflets of 30cm (1') long or more. They and the stems are soft, aromatic and incredibly flavoursome, with an onion / roasted garlic flavour and other distinctive spicy hints. They are mostly cooked (which doesn't take long), often in stir-fries and with eggs, or they can be added to stews and soups. They can also be blanched and used in salads, or dried, ground and used as a spice. In China, toon is also grown in punnets (like mustard or cress) and whole young seedlings used – these are tender and have a more delicate flavour. The seeds are sprouted in the same way as alfalfa.

The fresh leaves are high in protein, vitamins B1, B2, C and E, calcium and iron.

Trees cultivated for leaves can be kept shrubby by harvesting and regular trimming, to keep them about 1.5m (5') high. They do not cast a heavy shade and can sometimes be underplanted with another crop.

Toon leaf pesto

Making pesto is the best way to capture the great taste and spring vibrancy of toon. Here are two variations: one Italian-style pesto for pasta, and one using Eastern flavours for noodles. Pesto can also be used to add flavour to sauces and stews, or to coat vegetables before roasting.

The quantities are approximate and should make one jar and roughly four servings, but ratios can be tweaked, depending on your preferences.

For pasta:

Large handful of toon leaves

2-3 tbsp olive oil

2-3 tbsp pine nuts

30g (1oz) grated Parmesan

2 garlic cloves

½ tsp salt

For noodles:

Large handful of toon leaves

2-3 tbsp sesame oil

2-3 tbsp raw peanuts or cashews

1 tbsp grated fresh ginger

2 garlic cloves

1 tsp sugar

½ tsp salt

Fresh green chilli (as preferred)

Food processor

Method for both types:
Wash and dry the toon shoots and pick off the leaves and softest stalks. Place all ingredients into a food processor and blend into a paste, adding more oil if necessary.

Taste the pesto to see if you are happy with the flavour and texture. Add ingredients as necessary and blend again.

Transfer the pesto into clean jars, label with the date and add a little more oil to the top to make a seal before putting on the lid. The pesto will keep for up to 2 weeks in the fridge and can also be frozen in plastic containers or freezer bags.

Columbine (*Aquilegia vulgaris*)

Better known as just aquilegia, this shade-loving perennial is common in many gardens for its ornamental flowers.

The fresh leaves are edible, with a soft texture and mild, slightly sweet flavour. Plants continue to put out fresh leaves for much of the growing season, slowing only in very dry spells. Pick the leaves when still mid-green, before they darken and start to get tough. Make sure they have no signs of mildew, which can sometimes be present in dry periods.

The leaves are mostly used in salads, though they can also be added to cooked recipes (late on, so as not to overcook). The flowers are also edible; best in salads, either mixed in or as a garnish on top. The petals are thin but slightly sweet. Pick in spring.

There are many garden varieties of columbine, some of which are true *A. vulgaris*, while others are hybrids of this with other *Aquilegia* species. It is possible that all the hybrids can be used similarly to the species, but this cannot be guaranteed, as only *A. vulgaris* is documented as an edible plant.

Note that the seeds and roots of aquilegia are poisonous and should never be eaten.

Spring forest salad

This salad is satisfying to gather, as you can imagine our ancestors gathering the same combination of leaves in the late spring for generations past. Depending on the season, not all of the leaves listed will be right for picking – the trick with the beech and hawthorn leaves is to catch them when they are new and soft. The sorrel, dandelion and columbine also benefit from being new and fresh, when their flavour is milder.

Serves 4

1 part apple mint
1 part dandelion leaves
1 part wood sorrel
3 parts beech leaves
3 parts columbine leaves
3 parts hawthorn leaves

Garnish:
Dandelion petals and/or columbine flowers

Dressing:
2 tbsp olive oil
¼ tsp salt

The ratios can be varied according to taste and availability, but this recipe gives rough proportions according to strength of flavour and texture. This salad benefits from just a light dressing of olive oil and salt to allow all of the flavours to emerge.

Other recipes using columbine: Columbine gin liqueur (Part 1, page 27).

Dandelion (*Taraxacum officinale*)

Everyone knows dandelion – usually as a weed in their garden. And although most people know that you can make wine from the flowers and use the leaves in salads, few actually do so. Perhaps it is the bitterness of the fresh leaves that puts people off. Top chefs are starting to use dandelion leaves, often wilting them over heat for a few seconds to remove most of the bitterness.

Like many plants with deep, extensive root systems, the dandelion manages to extract many minerals from the soil and accumulate them in its leaves and roots. The leaves are high in iron, magnesium, phosphorus, copper, calcium, potassium and manganese; in vitamins A, C, E, K and B6; and in Thiamin and Riboflavin.

The younger leaves can be used from spring to autumn (winter too, in mild regions) but in very dry spells they get increasingly bitter. The flowers are picked in spring, when dandelion-rich fields can yield a good harvest very quickly. The roots are usually harvested in winter but can be lifted at any time of year, and are traditionally roasted to make a bitter coffee-type beverage.

Patrick Whitefield's spring salad

Patrick Whitefield is well known in the perma-culture arena: he has been teaching and consulting for the best part of 20 years, and is the author of a number of books. He keeps a log of the salads that work well and has contributed this one, and another for summer (page 143) to our collection. This salad should be picked in late April.

Bronze fennel leaf

Chicory

Dandelion

Garlic cress

Herb patience

Lamb's lettuce

Land cress

Lettuce

Mint

Musk mallow

Ramsons

Turkish rocket

Winter purslane

There are lots of strong flavours in this mix, so the milder, bulkier leaves, such as lettuce, lamb's lettuce, musk mallow and purslane, are important and should be included in bigger quantities than the stronger leaves, such as Turkish rocket, dandelion and land cress. The mint and fennel give a sweet contrast to the peppery leaves, and the ramsons is the linchpin that ties all the flavours together.

A bit of grated carrot or chopped tomato is always a good way to make an overly serious salad more acceptable to people with delicate taste!

Fennel (*Foeniculum vulgare*)

Another deep-rooted perennial, with distinctive feathery foliage and typical umbellifer-type flowers. Fennel has a great anise-type flavour which does not overpower. The herb fennel is different from Florence fennel, which is a biennial grown for the swollen lower stem to use as a vegetable.

The finely cut leaves and young stems can be harvested all though the growing season, though as the plants flower they can get a bit untidy. Traditionally, fennel leaves have often been used in fish recipes, sausages, salads and pastas.

Being deep-rooted, fennel accumulates many minerals in its aerial parts: leaves and stems are high in calcium, iron, magnesium, phosphorus, copper, potassium and manganese, among others; they also contain vitamin C and niacin. The seeds are high in the same minerals.

The flowers have the same flavour as the leaves and stems, and can themselves be used in early autumn. The seeds (both green and dried) are of course also widely used, both in cooking and to make a pleasant tea. The leaves can be dried – though they do lose some flavour – and then crushed and used as a spice. The ripe seeds retain their flavour well when stored.

Pan-fried sea bass with fennel & puréed sorrel

Serves 2

3 tbsp chopped fresh fennel leaf

2 large handfuls of shredded sorrel leaves

30g (1oz) butter

1 tbsp olive oil

1 medium fennel bulb, finely cut

1 medium onion, halved and finely sliced

2 sea bass fillets

Salt and pepper

Melt half the butter in a large frying pan and add the olive oil. Add the fennel bulb and onion and fry on a medium heat for 3 minutes until they have softened and become translucent.

Prepare the sea bass fillets by rinsing with cold water, then patting them dry with kitchen paper and sprinkling a little salt and black pepper on each side.

Push the onion and fennel to the sides of the frying pan and add the remaining butter in the centre. When the butter begins to bubble add the fish, skin-side down and fry on a medium heat for 4 minutes. Reduce to a low heat and turn the fillets over. Fry for a further 2 minutes then place the fish on to a warm plate.

Quickly add the shredded sorrel and fennel leaf to the frying pan and cover on a low heat for 2-3 minutes, stirring occasionally, until wilted. The sorrel leaves will form a purée when wilted and mixed with the remnants of butter, oil and fish juices in the pan. Season, stir well and remove from the heat.

Serve the fillets on top of or beside the onions and fennel, with a spoonful of sorrel purée on top.

Other recipes using fennel: Cardoon & lamb tagine (page 112); Mallow leaf dolmades (page 128); Plantain & broad bean tabbouleh (page 133); Siberian purslane salad with ramsons and hazelnut dressing (page 217); Moroccan-style aerial yams (page 227); Pickled Chinese artichokes (Part 1, page 25); Vinegar infusions (Part 1, page 26).

Giant butterbur
(*Petasites japonicus*)

Also known as fuki; sweet coltsfoot

This plant resembles a large rhubarb, with thick leaf stalks and large rounded leaves. The leaf stalks are a popular vegetable in Japan, used mainly in stews and soups or as a side vegetable. They are high in calcium, potassium, copper, manganese and vitamin C, with a very distinctive flavour: sweet and aromatic and not dissimilar to celery, but stronger. The stalks are harvested in spring; the leaves discarded. It is best to cut them for just a few weeks and then allow the replacement shoots to grow to sustain the plant.

The cut stalks store in a fridge for about 1 week. Because of the tough fibres running through the stem, they are usually prepared as follows. Cut into lengths to fit into a saucepan, add to boiling water and boil for 3-5 minutes. Strain and rinse in cold water to cool. Peel the fibres off using fingernails, a vegetable peeler or the edge of a knife, working your way around the circumference of the chopped stalk end. If using alone as a side vegetable, the fuki will need an additional 5 minutes of boiling or steaming.

Sautéd fuki & carrot with orange & rosemary

Serves 4

280g (10oz) fuki, chopped into 5cm (2") lengths

1 orange, juice and zest

1 tsp sugar

2 tsp chopped fresh rosemary

Salt and pepper

200g (7oz) carrots, sliced lengthways and chopped into 5cm (2") lengths

30g (1oz) butter

Parboil the fuki and carrot pieces for 5 minutes, then strain and allow to cool and dry. Remove any tough fibres from the fuki pieces if necessary.

Grate the zest from the orange, then juice it and place zest and juice in a mixing bowl. Add the sugar, rosemary, salt and pepper to the bowl. Add the fuki and carrot pieces to the liquid and mix well, ensuring the vegetables are well covered.

Melt the butter in a large, heavy-based frying pan. When it begins to sizzle, add the vegetables to the pan, spread out evenly, and fry for 5 minutes. Turn the vegetables and fry for a further 5 minutes. Repeat this until they are browned on both sides and the liquid has caramelised.

Serve as a side vegetable.

Fuki casserole

Serves 4

200g (7oz) fuki stalks

1 large onion, diced

A little vegetable oil

½ tsp ground cumin

1 tsp ground coriander

1 400g (14oz) tin chickpeas, rinsed and drained

3 medium carrots, diced

200g (7oz) potatoes, diced

3 celery sticks, cut into 2cm (¾") chunks

1l (1¾ pints / 35fl oz) vegetable stock

Salt and pepper

¼ tsp allspice

1 tsp dried thyme

Preheat the oven to 160°C (320°F / Gas Mark 2½)

Chop the fuki into lengths that will fit into a saucepan. Place in the pan and cover with boiling water, then bring to the boil and simmer for 4 minutes.

Strain and rinse with cold water. Remove the fibres as described above. Once peeled, chop the fuki into 2cm (¾") chunks.

In a large saucepan fry the onion in a little vegetable oil for 3 minutes. Add the cumin and coriander and cook for a further 2 minutes. Add the chickpeas and all of the vegetables to the pan and pour over the stock, bring to the boil and remove from the heat. Add salt, pepper, the allspice and the dried thyme and stir well.

Transfer the ingredients to a 2l (3½ pint) casserole dish and ensure there is enough liquid to cover all the vegetables – if not, add a little more stock. There should be at least 2.5cm (1") between the liquid and the top of the dish to prevent liquid escaping while cooking. Cover and put in the centre of the oven for 50-60 minutes.

Serve with mashed potato or rice, or as a chunky broth with a hunk of bread.

Good King Henry
(*Chenopodium bonus-henricus*)

Sometimes confused with the weed 'fat hen', to which it is related, Good King Henry is actually found rather rarely in the wild in the UK. (It is not named after an English King Henry, but after a Teutonic elf from folklore.) It is an unassuming long-lived perennial with almost triangular-shaped leaves and spikes of flowers.

The plant is used as a vegetable in two ways. The leaves and leaf stalks can be used like spinach right through the growing season, and are excellent in stir-fries. The leaves can be used layered in pasta dishes, for example. Also, the new shoots coming through the soil in spring can be cut and used like asparagus (indeed, another name for the plant is 'poor man's asparagus'). Only the first shoots should be taken and the later ones left to grow to sustain the plant. It is better to cultivate a patch of several plants and harvest a few shoots or leaves from each, rather than strip a whole plant, which can weaken it substantially.

Good King Henry is high in protein, potassium, phosphorus, magnesium and vitamins A and C.

Good King Henry stuffed mushrooms

Serves 4

350g (12oz) Good King Henry leaves
30g (1oz) butter
2 large onions, finely chopped
3 garlic cloves, crushed
500ml (18fl oz) single cream
80g (2¾oz) Gruyère cheese, grated
8 large flat mushrooms
Salt and pepper

Preheat the oven to 180°C (350°F / Gas Mark 4)

Melt the butter in a saucepan, add the onions and fry for 5 minutes until soft and golden. Add the crushed garlic and fry for another minute.

Rinse the Good King Henry leaves, but don't dry them. Transfer them to a large saucepan, put on the lid and place over a low heat for 2-3 minutes until the leaves have wilted. Add the leaves to the onions and stir in. Add the cream and half the Gruyère, return the pan to a medium heat and bring to almost boiling, stirring continuously. Turn off the heat before the mixture boils.

Wipe the mushrooms clean and remove the stalks. Lay the mushrooms upside down (gills upwards) on a greased baking tray and spoon the mixture evenly between them. Sprinkle the remaining cheese on top of each stuffed mushroom and finish with a twist of black pepper.

Place into the top of the oven and bake for 20-30 minutes, until browned.

Serve straight away as a starter or main.

Stir-fried Good King Henry

Serves 4

400g (14oz) Good King Henry leaves
Sesame or vegetable oil
40g (1½oz) sweet cicely seeds
Pinch of salt

Heat a little oil in a wok or frying pan to a good heat, add Good King Henry leaves and fry for 2-3 minutes, stirring constantly. Add the sweet cicely seeds and a pinch of salt halfway through.

Hop (*Humulus lupulus*)

Hops are perennial twining climbers, and can reach 2-6m (6'6"-20') in height each year (depending on the variety), before dying down to a rootstock in winter. Once established, the plants usually sucker outwards and put up many more shoots than are required for a crop of 'cones' (the female flowers used in brewing and herbal medicine).

Hop shoots make an excellent spring vegetable, and are relished in many regions. When raw they have tiny hooks on the stems, like cleavers (*Galium aparine*), but once cooked they have a pleasant texture and a nice, slightly nutty flavour.

Hop plants have extensive root systems which are very efficient at getting nutrients from the soil. Aerial parts, such as the shoots, are very high in calcium and potassium, and also high in phosphorus, magnesium and other minerals. The shoots do not contain the complex aromatic compounds that are present in hop flowers, hence do not have the medicinal properties of the flowers.

Any excess shoots are cut in spring and summer over many months – just cut or pinch off about 20cm (8") from the top, either at ground level or from higher up. Established plants can yield many dozens of shoots. Once cut, store quickly in a fridge, otherwise they will wilt; they will keep refrigerated for 4-5 days. They are not usually dried or preserved.

Hop shoots with lemon & capers

Serves 4

200g (7oz) hop shoots, cut into 5cm (2") lengths
30g (1oz) butter
Half a lemon, juice and zest
1 garlic clove, crushed
Salt and black pepper
3 tsp capers

Bring a saucepan of water to the boil and drop the hop shoots in with a pinch of salt. Reduce the heat and simmer for 2 minutes. Strain and allow the shoots to steam and dry a little.

In a frying pan, melt the butter on a low heat and add the lemon juice and zest, garlic, salt and pepper. Transfer the hops to the pan and gently sauté for 2 minutes. Rinse the capers in cold water and add them to the pan and fry for a further 5 minutes.

Serve as a side vegetable with fish, or stir into hot tagliatelli with olive oil as a light meal.

Hop shoots are also nice on their own as a steamed vegetable – serve with butter, mayonnaise or a sauce.

Grilled haddock with hop shoots

Serves 2

100g (3½oz) hop shoots

1 red pepper, sliced lengthways into thick strips

4 fresh tomatoes, chopped into chunks

4 garlic cloves, peeled

2 tsp paprika

1 medium-sized haddock, filleted into two, boned and skinned

A little olive oil

1 tbsp balsamic vinegar

Salt and black pepper

Place the peppers skin-side up on to a foil-covered grill pan. Place the tomatoes around the peppers and the garlic cloves among the peppers and tomatoes. Sprinkle the contents of the grill pan with 1 tsp of paprika and place under a high grill for 5 minutes.

Wash the haddock fillets and pat dry. Brush with a little olive oil and season. Place the fillets skin-side up in the middle of the grill pan, pushing the tomatoes and peppers to aside to make space. Grill for 3-4 minutes, then turn the fillets over. Sprinkle 1 tsp of paprika over the fish and the vegetables and replace under a medium-hot grill for 4-6 minutes, or until the fish is cooked through. Be careful not to over-cook the fish as it will become dry and tough.

Half-fill a large saucepan with water and bring to the boil. Add a good pinch of salt and reduce to a simmer. Drop the hop shoots into the water and simmer for 3 minutes. Strain and place on to kitchen paper or a clean tea towel to dry. Take the fish and vegetables out from the grill and put the fillets of haddock straight on to hot dinner plates. Arrange the hop shoots on top on the fish and take some of the red pepper strips from the grill pan and arrange around the fish. Transfer the remaining vegetables to a saucepan and add the balsamic vinegar. Stir as you bring the mixture to the boil and then remove from the heat and spoon over the hops and fish.

Serve immediately with boiled new potatoes.

Hostas (*Hosta* spp.)

Hostas are woodland perennials, most originating from Asia, and they are well-known ornamentals in Europe and North America. Amazingly, very few people in these parts know that most – probably all – hostas can be used as a vegetable. They are commonly eaten in some parts of Asia, particularly in Japan.

The shoots / leaf clusters are eaten in salads or, more usually, cooked in various ways – steamed, stir-fried, etc. There is little information available on their nutritional content but, like many spring shoots, they are likely to be high in minerals. Certainly they are relished by animals, including rabbits and deer.

Very useful plants for growing in shady conditions, hostas have a reputation for being susceptible to slugs and snails. It helps, therefore, to grow the larger, most robust species and varieties (e.g. *H. sieboldiana*, 'Big Daddy' or 'Blue Umbrella'), which soon outgrow any mollusc problems. The new shoots are not usually damaged at all in any case.

The shoots are harvested in spring soon after they push through the ground, before the leaves start to unfurl: at this time the leaf cluster looks a bit like green chicory chicons. They can be harvested over several weeks, including the entire first flush of shoots from an established patch, after which the plants should be left to recover.

Hosta & chicken coconut soup

This soup is rich and full of flavour, yet light and aromatic. Quick and easy to prepare, it makes an ideal lunch or a great starter to awaken the taste buds. It's also a good way to use up leftover chicken from a Sunday roast, although you can use raw chicken sliced into fine strips and seared if you don't have any cooked to hand.

Serves 4

100g (3½oz) hostas

1l (1¾ pints / 35fl oz) chicken stock

340ml (12fl oz) coconut milk

2 tbsp lime juice

2 tbsp Chinese fish sauce

1 tsp sugar

1 tbsp fresh ginger, finely grated

150g (5¼oz) cooked chicken, cut into small pieces

80g (2¾oz) sweetcorn

3 tbsp chopped fresh coriander leaves

100g (3½oz) rice noodles

Salt and pepper

Take a large saucepan and pour in the chicken stock, coconut milk, lime juice, fish sauce, sugar, ginger and chicken. Stir together and bring to the boil over a medium heat. Reduce to a low heat and simmer for 10 minutes.

Rinse the hosta shoots and remove any tough ends or bad leaves. Where possible, keep the shoots whole. Add the hostas, sweetcorn and half the coriander; simmer for a further 5 minutes.

Break the noodles into 2 or 3 lengths and add them to the soup. Rice noodles usually take between 2 and 5 minutes to cook, so add them at the end of cooking according to the instructions on the packet.

Remove from the heat, stir in the remaining coriander, season to taste and serve. The noodles will continue to absorb the liquid and become swollen and soft, so this soup is best eaten straight away.

For an extra kick, try adding a little finely chopped fresh chilli at the beginning.

Japanese hostas with shrimps

Serves 4

200g (7oz) hosta shoots
500g (1lb 2oz) shrimps (small prawns)
2 tbsp sesame or sunflower oil
1 red pepper, sliced into thin strips
1 large carrot, sliced into thin strips

Marinade
4 tbsp rice or white wine vinegar
2 tbsp soy sauce
2 garlic cloves, crushed
2.5cm (2") piece fresh ginger, finely grated

Garnish
2 tbsp sesame seeds, toasted

Begin by making a marinade for the shrimps. Place the vinegar and soy sauce into a bowl and add the garlic and ginger. Stir well and allow to steep for 20 minutes. Strain the mixture through a sieve into another bowl and add the shrimps, ensuring they are well covered with the marinade.

Wash the hosta shoots and remove any tough ends or shrivelled leaves. Heat the oil in a wok, add the hostas, peppers and carrots and stir-fry on a high heat for 5 minutes or until the hosta leaves have softened and become dark and glossy. Transfer the shrimps and marinade to the wok and stir-fry for another 2 minutes.

Serve on a bed of rice or noodles and sprinkle with the toasted sesame seeds.

Try this with other seasonal greens from the forest garden, such as Siberian purslane, hop shoots, alexanders or Solomon's seal.

Ice plant (*Sedum spectabile*)

Ice plant and orpine (see page 89) are sometimes separated off botanically from the tiny-leaved sedums because they have large fleshy green leaves and very large white, pink or reddish flowers, which are much loved by bees.

Ice plant is a useful salad plant, with succulent leaves and a mild, fresh, slightly peppery flavour. It is best used as bulk in green salads and can be used to give balance when used with strong-flavoured ingredients. Two examples of recipes that make use of these attributes are given overleaf.

The plants like well-drained conditions and prefer sun, but will tolerate some light shade.

The leaves are available to harvest from spring through to autumn, although in hot summer periods they sometimes get a little bitter.

Ice plant with peanuts & coconut

Serves 4

200g (7oz) ice plant leaves
80g (2¾oz) musk mallow leaves
4 tbsp chopped fresh sweet cicely leaf
Juice of half a lime
1 tbsp sunflower oil
70g (2½oz) desiccated coconut
80g (2¾oz) peanuts, toasted and coarsely chopped

Rinse and dry the ice plant leaves. Leave half of the leaves whole, and roughly chop the other half.

Roughly chop all but 3 or 4 of the mallow leaves and put the whole leaves to one side.

Arrange the whole ice plant leaves around the sides and base of a salad bowl. In a separate bowl mix together the chopped ice plant, sweet cicely and mallow leaves. Combine the lime and oil and drizzle over the leaves. Add the coconut and toasted peanuts. Toss the ingredients together well and transfer to the salad bowl, leaving a fringe of whole leaves visible around the edge. Garnish with the whole mallow leaves and serve.

Ice plant raita

200g (7oz) ice plant leaves
500g (1lb 1¾oz) plain yogurt
1 tsp lemon juice
2 tbsp chopped fresh mint
Pinch of salt
1 tsp whole cumin seeds

Optional:
1 tsp caster sugar

Garnish:
Cumin seeds

Chop the ice plant leaves into 5mm (⅛") strips and add to a mixing bowl. Add the yogurt, lemon juice, mint and salt, and sugar if desired.

In a frying pan gently toast the cumin seeds for 2 minutes on a low heat, until the aroma is released. Gently crush the toasted seeds with a pestle and mortar.

Keep a pinch of seeds aside to garnish and add the rest to the other ingredients. Stir together well and transfer to a serving bowl. Sprinkle with the remaining cumin seeds and serve with Indian meals or a salad buffet.

Lesser stitchwort
(*Stellaria graminea*)

Lesser stitchwort is one of those native plants that abounds in hedgerows but that many folk never notice unless it is in flower – showing its small, neat, round white blossoms in spring. It is closely related to the well-known weed and wild edible chickweed (*S. media*).

The leaves and long, thread-like stems of stitchwort can be eaten raw or cooked, and have a pleasant nutty flavour and green freshness. When cooked, the tangle of stems is reminiscent of spaghetti. The recipe overleaf, which substitutes stitchwort for pasta, is based on a simple, classic Italian dish.

The plant grows with long thread-like stems, dotted with leaves all along, and prefers semi-shaded conditions, so is very easy to fit into a forest garden environment.

The leaves and young stems are available to harvest right through from spring to autumn, although as the season progresses only a few inches of the tips of the shoots are tender enough to eat raw.

Stitchwort aglio e olio

Serves 4

200g (7oz) stitchwort
3 garlic cloves, crushed
100ml (3½fl oz) olive oil
2 tbsp chopped fresh flat leaf parsley
1 tbsp lemon juice
Salt and pepper

Optional:
50g (1¾oz) grated Parmesan

Rinse the stitchwort and remove tough ends, but not flowers or buds. Bring a large pan of water to the boil with a pinch of salt and drop in the stitchwort. Boil for 5 minutes, then strain and return to the pan.

Add all the other ingredients except the seasoning and Parmesan (if using) to the pan and stir-fry on a low heat for 2 minutes. Remove from the heat, stir in the Parmesan, season and serve.

Try stitchwort raw as a salad base or with a mixture of leaves. The firm, crunchy stems work well with soft avocado and fresh, juicy tomatoes with a balsamic dressing and a few mixed seeds tossed in.

Orpine (*Sedum telephium*)

Orpine leaves have a wonderful crisp succulence that makes them great for a salad base. The flavour is mild and sweet with no bitterness, and the combined texture and flavour has a similar quality to cucumber and makes them a good 'bulk' salad leaf. The simple recipes overleaf combine the leaves with stronger, more acidic flavours to create fresh, crunchy salads that are tasty and balanced.

This plant is a drought-tolerant herbaceous perennial that likes well-drained conditions and prefers full sun, though it tolerates some light shade. Likes other sedums it is an excellent bee plant, but the white flowers are not as showy as those of ice plant (see page 85). There are named ornamental varieties with different-coloured leaves and flowers.

The leaves are available to harvest from spring through to autumn, although in hot summer periods they sometimes get a little bitter. You can pick individual leaves off stems (older ones can be fine) or pinch off the tender shoot tips – new side shoots are put out a few weeks later.

Orpine & tomato salad

Serves 4

200g (7oz) orpine leaves
6 medium fresh tomatoes, diced
Half a medium red onion, finely chopped
1 tbsp chopped fresh mint leaves
1 tbsp chopped fresh sweet cicely leaf
1 tbsp balsamic vinegar
½ tsp sugar
2 tbsp olive oil
Pinch of salt

Arrange the orpine leaves around the inside of a salad bowl. Mix together the tomatoes, onion and herbs and place in the bowl on top of the orpine.

Whisk together the balsamic vinegar, sugar, olive oil and salt and drizzle over the salad to serve.

American-style orpine salad

This is a popular salad made with cucumbers in the USA.

Serves 4

200g (7oz) orpine leaves, cut into 5mm (⅛") slices
2 tbsp boiling water
50g (1¾oz) white sugar
1 tbsp white wine vinegar
4 tbsp mayonnaise
6 chopped fresh spearmint leaves
½ tsp salt

Mix the boiling water, sugar and vinegar in a bowl and stir until the sugar has dissolved. Add the mayonnaise and mix together well. Mix the orpine leaves and spearmint into the dressing and refrigerate for 30 minutes before serving.

Ostrich fern
(*Matteuccia struthiopteris*)

Also known as shuttlecock fern

Well known in North America as a vegetable, this is almost unknown as an edible else-where. The crops are the 'fiddleheads' – the young shoots that emerge quite early in spring, with leaves still tightly curled, about 5-7cm (2-3") high.

The fiddleheads are tender and tasty when raw, and work well tossed into salads, especially with sweet flavours such as sweetcorn and pepper. However, occasionally they can cause an upset stomach if not cooked. When cooked they have a light, crunchy texture and a delicate flavour, between broccoli and asparagus, and are delicious on their own or as a side vegetable, especially with fish. They also go well with eggs or light pasta dishes. They are high in vitamins A and C, and Niacin.

As plants become established the number of shoots increases; they also spread by rhizomes. They much prefer shady and moist conditions. The fiddleheads can be harvested intensively for about 3 weeks, after which the ferns are left to grow, reaching up to 1m (3') high.

Fiddlehead fritters

Serves 4

100g (3½oz) ostrich fern shoots
Vegetable oil

Dip:
200ml (7oz) Greek-style yogurt
1 tbsp chopped fresh parsley
1 tbsp chopped capers
1 tsp lemon juice

Batter:
30g (1oz) self-raising flour
Salt and pepper
1 egg
150ml (5¼fl oz) water
1 tsp olive oil

To make the dip, simply add all ingredients together and stir well, then place in a dipping bowl and keep cool.

Wash and pat dry the fern shoots and trim any discoloured or tough ends.

Sift the flour into a mixing bowl and add seasoning. Make a small dip in the middle of the flour and break the egg into the dip. Add the water and olive oil and gradually whisk the liquids into the surrounding flour until you have a smooth batter. The mixture should be quite runny to form a light and crispy coating for the fern shoots. If it seems too thick you can add more water; experiment by dipping a fern shoot into the mixture – it should cling to the fern but not smother it.

In a heavy-based saucepan add 2.5cm (1") of vegetable oil and place over a medium heat. Add drops of batter to the oil as it heats to check the temperature. When the batter droplets begin to fizz, the temperature is right; turn the heat down a little to maintain this temperature and don't allow the oil to get too hot. You may need to adjust the heat as you cook.

One by one dip the fern shoots into the batter and drop them into the oil. Have a plate with 2-3 layers of kitchen paper on top to place the fritters on to when they are done. The fritters will take only about 2 minutes to cook to a golden brown, crispy finish. Don't overcrowd the pan, so you are able to turn the fritters, and keep an eye on them – they may cook at different rates, depending on their size.

The kitchen paper will help to absorb excess oil and you may wish to pat them on top as well. The fritters will be very hot initially but cool down quickly, and are best served fresh and hot. Quickly transfer them to a clean plate and serve with the dip as a starter or nibbles.

Try this with other dips, such as sweet chilli sauce or a simple mixture of soy sauce and lemon juice. You could also add other complementary vegetables to the batter – red pepper and baby sweetcorn, for example.

Ostrich fern shoots with trout & new potatoes

Serves 4

80g (2¾oz) ostrich fern shoots
1 kg (2lb 3oz) new potatoes
30g (1oz) butter
1 garlic clove, crushed
100ml (3½fl oz) dry white wine
100ml (3½fl oz) vegetable or fish stock
1 tsp lemon juice
1 tbsp chopped fresh parsley
Salt and coarse black pepper
2 smoked trout fillets, skin removed

Wash the new potatoes and chop any larger ones so that they are about the same size as the smallest whole potatoes. Add them to a pan of boiling water with a pinch of salt and boil for 10-12 minutes, or until the largest potatoes drop off smoothly when you push a fork into them. Strain, replace the lid and keep warm while you cook the ferns.

Melt the butter in a non-stick pan over a medium heat. Add the fern shoots and crushed garlic and gently sauté for 3 minutes. Add the wine and the stock and bring to the boil. Simmer for 8 minutes, stirring occasionally until the sauce has reduced and thickened a little. Remove from the heat and stir in the lemon juice, parsley, salt and pepper.

Take the smoked trout fillets, break them into bite-sized flakes and add them to the pan. Add the cooked potatoes and place over low heat for 2 minutes to warm through, gently stirring the ingredients together and ensuring they are evenly covered with sauce.

Serve hot as a light lunch.

Try ostrich fern shoots as a side vegetable, lightly sautéd in butter with a good twist of black pepper and a pinch of salt.

Alternatively try them raw in a simple salad with Siberian purslane, ramsons, red pepper and sweetcorn with a balsamic dressing.

Ramsons (*Allium ursinum*)

Also known as wild garlic

Ramsons is hard to miss in spring if you are near it in woods, where it often forms large colonies and has a strong garlic smell. Superbly adapted to deciduous woodland, ramsons starts growing very early (sometimes in late February), flowers in May, sets seed in June and has usually vanished by July, dying back to a thin, almost cylindrical perennial bulb.

The leaves can be eaten from February to May – they become untidy when the plants flower – and have a strong garlic flavour.

Like many in this family (and true garlic itself), ramsons contains, among other things, sulphur compounds that are believed to boost the immune system and act as antibiotics. It is also high in vitamin C.

It is easy to establish in forest gardens, though its self-seeding habit may need some controlling. All parts of the plant can be eaten, but the bulbs are very small and hardly worth the trouble.

Ramsons pesto

2 large handfuls of ramsons leaves, washed
500ml (18fl oz) olive oil
150g (5¼oz) walnuts, pine nuts or hazelnuts
100g (3½oz) Parmesan cheese, grated
1 tsp fine sea salt

Stick blender or liquidiser

Pour the olive oil into a large jug (if using a stick blender) or a liquidiser. Add a handful of ramsons followed by the nuts, cheese and salt. Blend until smooth (or to the texture you like), then add more ramsons, a few at a time, until you have a thick paste. Taste the pesto to see if it needs more salt, then transfer it to sterilised glass jars, or plastic storage containers if it is to be frozen. In jars it will keep in the fridge for up to 2 weeks if you pour a little olive oil on top of the paste to form a seal and keep out mould. In the freezer it will keep for 3 months, and after defrosting will keep in the fridge for 1-2 weeks – remember to add oil to the top.

Pesto can be stirred into pasta, used to flavour stews and sauces, or spread on to bread and grilled to make bruschetta.

Try a dairy-free version of this recipe by leaving out the Parmesan and using cashews in place of or alongside other nuts. When blended with the oil, the cashews break down to become soft and creamy, giving the pesto a rich texture and flavour without the addition of cheese.

Ramsons leaves can be used in moderation in salads, or added late into cooked recipes – the flavour dissipates rapidly on cooking so you don't want to overcook. The flowers can also be eaten, and are particularly good in salads.

Other recipes using ramsons: Solomon's seal gnocchi (page 102).

Rhubarbs (*Rheum* spp.)

The rhubarb family contains many species; the 'normal' cultivated one is in fact a hybrid of several. It appears that the leaf stalks of all species can be eaten. Although rhubarb is treated like a fruit in the UK, it is of course a leaf stem vegetable, and can be used in many ways other than being merely stewed with sugar.

Rhubarbs are large, robust, perennial plants, with large leaves borne on thick stalks. The stalks of different species have different flavours: those of *R. australe*, for example, are apple-flavoured, while *R. palmatum* stalks have a distinctly gooseberry tang. They are all acidic when raw due to the oxalic acid content, which can build up during the growing season. This is why it is traditional to harvest rhubarb mainly in spring, until about mid-summer. Oxalic acid is found in many other edible crops, including sorrels, spinach, beet, chard, Good King Henry and oca. Although in theory it can lock up calcium in the body, you would have to eat a good deal (several kilos per week) for a long time to cause problems, and most plants containing oxalic acid also have high levels of calcium, which act as an offset. Also, any cooking minimises the effects.

Traditionally, rhubarb is cooked with sweet cicely leaves, as a sweetening agent. It is high in vitamins C and K, calcium, potassium and manganese.

Rhubarb & beetroot salad

Serves 4

400g (14oz) rhubarb, cut into 1cm (⅜") chunks

80g (2¾oz) baby spinach leaves

2 medium beetroot, peeled and grated

1 tbsp brown sugar

4 tbsp walnut pieces

1 tsp honey

1 tsp wholegrain mustard

100ml (3½fl oz) olive oil

Arrange the baby spinach leaves between 4 plates. Divide the beetroot into four, making a pile on top of the spinach on each plate.

Place the rhubarb into a saucepan and add the brown sugar and enough cold water to cover. Bring to the boil and reduce to a simmer for 3 minutes, or until the rhubarb is soft but still firm and holding its form. Remove from the heat and strain off, retaining the cooking liquid. Arrange the rhubarb chunks on top of the beetroot on each plate and sprinkle the walnuts on top.

Add the honey and mustard to the hot cooking liquid and stir in until fully dissolved. This salad works well warm or cold, so if you want a warm salad, whisk in the oil immediately, drizzle over the salad plates and serve. If you would prefer a cold salad, put the plates and the dressing mix in the fridge until you are ready, and whisk in the olive oil just before serving.

Spiced rhubarb fool

This is a simple, traditional pudding with a twist, which can be whipped up literally in minutes! The stewed rhubarb is spiced with sweet cicely seeds, allspice and orange zest, which are complemented by the cool, smooth base of custard and cream.

Serves 4

500g (1lb 1¾oz) rhubarb, cut into 2.5cm (1") chunks
1 orange, juice and zest
1 tbsp caster sugar
½ tsp allspice
2 tbsp young sweet cicely seeds
300ml (10½fl oz) whipping cream
300ml (10½fl oz) custard

Garnish:
A few sweet cicely seeds

Put the rhubarb pieces into a saucepan and add the orange juice and zest, caster sugar, allspice and sweet cicely seeds. Cover and place over a low heat, stirring occasionally, until the rhubarb has become pulpy. Remove from the heat and put aside to cool.

Whip the cream and gently fold in the custard until you have an even mixture. Fold half of the cooled rhubarb into the custard cream – you can mix it completely or leave streaks or 'ripples' of the fruit running through it.

Remove 4 tablespoons of the fruit mixture and put to one side. Take 4 large dessert glasses and spoon a quarter of the remaining fruit into the bottom of each. Next, spoon in a quarter of the creamy mixture into each glass, on top of the fruit layer. Finish the top with a tablespoon of fruit and a few sweet cicely seeds.

Return to the fridge for 20 minutes and serve with shortbread fingers, or just as it is.

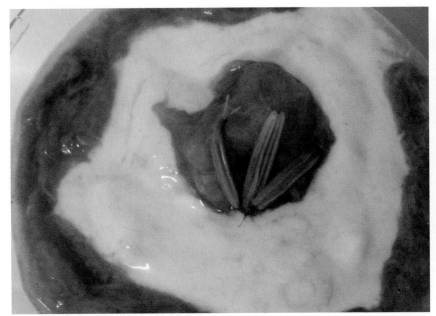

Solomon's seals
(*Polygonatum* spp.)

Solomon's seals are shade-loving perennials with arching shoots that grow from a fleshy, creeping rootstock that can expand to form colonies. The species range from 60cm to 2m (2' to 6'6") high and the young shoots of all can be eaten. Those of the taller species tend to be thicker. The shoots are deliciously sweet and are cooked in the same way as asparagus, either steamed for a few minutes or sautéd in butter. It is best not to overcook them as they are best 'al dente', with a little crunch.

These shoots have become one of Martin's favourite spring shoot crops in recent years. They emerge early in spring – in April, in Devon – and are harvested at 20-30cm (8-12") high, before the leaf cluster at the top opens out. If you wait too long, the opening leaf cluster becomes bitter and the whole shoots starts to get tough.

You can take most of the first flush of shoots as a crop, but then new ones should be allowed to develop, to allow the plants to recover and gain energy to store in their rhizomes later in the year.

Solomon's seal & Egyptian onion tart

This delicious quiche is a real treat and a pretty dish to serve to guests: quick and easy to make, especially if you use ready-made frozen pastry. However, if you like to make your own pastry you can always make large batches when you have the time, divide it into convenient-sized balls, wrap it in cling film and freeze it, ready for when you're in more of a hurry.

Serves 4-6

30g (1oz) Solomon's seal shoots

500g ready-made all-butter shortcrust pastry

3 eggs, beaten

40ml (1½fl oz) milk

30ml (1fl oz) double cream

Salt and pepper

100g (3½oz) Cheddar cheese, grated

1 large slice of thick-cut honey-roast ham, coarsely chopped

4 Egyptian onion leaves, chopped into rounds

Baking beans (dried beans or lentils)

A 25cm (10") flan dish.

Preheat the oven to 180°C (350°F, Gas Mark 4)

Wash the Solomon's seal, removing any tips that have begun to form flower buds, as well as any papery sheaths around the base of the shoots. Cut to lengths of about 15cm (6") and place into a large saucepan with a pinch of salt. Cover with water and bring to the boil, then reduce to a simmer for 2 minutes. Strain and put to one side.

On a flour-dusted surface, roll the pastry into a circle of about 35cm (14") in diameter and 5-10mm (⅛-⅜") thick, turning regularly to avoid sticking. Lift the pastry by draping it over the rolling pin and lay it over the flan dish. Lifting the edges of the sheet of pastry, gently tuck it into the corners of the dish, working your way around the circumference. Slice off the excess with a knife and prick the bottom with a fork. To get a nice, crispy base it pays to 'blind bake' the pastry casing. Place a layer of foil or baking parchment over the pastry and fill with baking beans, which will provide weight to prevent the pastry from lifting away from the bottom of the dish as it cooks. Bake for 20 minutes.

Whisk together the eggs, milk, cream, salt and pepper. Take the pastry case from the oven and remove the baking beans and foil. Sprinkle two-thirds of the cheese over the bottom, followed by most of the ham and Egyptian onions. Arrange the Solomon's seal on top and then sprinkle over the remaining ham, onions and cheese. Pour over the egg mixture evenly and return the flan dish to the oven. Cook for a further 25-30 minutes until the egg is set in the middle and the top has browned lightly.

Serve with salad for lunch or with potatoes and greens as a main meal.

101

Solomon's seal gnocchi

Serves 4

100g (3½oz) Solomon's seal, cut into 1cm (⅜") rounds
1 tbsp olive oil
30g (1oz) butter
200g (7oz) chestnut mushrooms, thinly sliced
6 Egyptian onion leaves, cut into 1cm (⅜") rounds
6 chopped fresh ramsons leaves
150ml (5¼fl oz) cream
50g (1¾oz) grated Parmesan
800g (1lb 12oz) gnocchi
Salt and pepper

Melt together the oil and butter in a saucepan and fry the Solomon's seal, mushrooms and Egyptian onions on a medium heat for 4 minutes.

Add the ramsons to the pan and fry for 1 minute. Turn to a low heat and add the cream and Parmesan. Stir in well and bring almost to the boil, then turn off the heat.

Bring a saucepan full of water to a rolling boil and add the gnocchi with a good pinch of salt and a dash of olive oil. Boil for 3 minutes, strain and add the

gnocchi to the other ingredients. Mix together well and serve immediately.

Solomon's seal shoots have a delicious sweet flavour and are great just steamed for a few minutes with butter or a sauce.

Stinging nettle (*Urtica dioica*)

Well known as a weed and wild edible, the stinging nettle is abundant in gardens, woods and fields throughout the land.

The top leaves that appear early in spring can be infused in hot water to make tea, wilted with butter as a side vegetable or incorporated into various dishes. The stings vanish once cooked. The leaves and soft green stalks can be treated much like spinach, and will wilt down in a similar way, so they can be added to stews, curries and soups at the last moment for a touch of spring green.

The simple but tasty soup recipe included here is a very easy way to use nettles, and you can really pack them into the pan. A nettle tea will nourish a human, and will also feed a plant with vital nitrogen for growth. Nettles are very high in vitamin A, and high in vitamin K, iron, zinc and calcium.

For human consumption, nettles are best gathered in springtime – picking the top few soft leaves of their first flush of growth, and wearing gloves of course!

Nettle, leek & spring onion quiche

Serves 4-6

One large (gloved) handful of nettles

30g (1oz) butter

1 large leek, cut into 1cm (⅜") rounds

2 spring onions or perennial onion leaves, cut into 1cm (⅜") rounds

5 ramsons leaves, coarsely chopped

80g (2¾oz) grated mature Cheddar cheese

3 tbsp crème fraîche

3 tbsp milk

4 beaten eggs

Salt and pepper

½ tsp dried tarragon

Pastry:

200g (7oz) self-raising flour

Pinch of salt

100g (3½oz) butter or margarine, at room temperature

Dash of milk

Baking beans (dried beans or lentils)

A 25cm (10") flan dish

Preheat the oven to 180°C (350°F / Gas Mark 4)

Grease and flour the flan dish and put to one side. Sift the flour into a mixing bowl and add the salt. Chop the butter or margarine into small pieces and work it into the flour with your fingertips to form a crumbly mixture, which should form a loose ball when squeezed together. Add a sprinkling of milk, a little at a time, and continue working the mixture until it forms a cohesive ball in your hand. Gather up all of the mixture and form one ball.

Dust a flat surface and a rolling pin with flour. Press the ball of pastry into a flat disc and roll it out, turning from time to time to prevent sticking, to a circle of roughly 30cm/12" in diameter. Carefully lift the pastry, draping it over the rolling pin, and lay it over the flan dish. Lift the edges and tuck the pastry into the corners of the dish. Slice off the excess with a knife and prick the base with a fork. Place a layer of foil or baking parchment over the pastry and fill with baking beans, which will provide weight to prevent the pastry from lifting away from the bottom of the dish as it cooks. Bake for 20 minutes, then remove the baking beans and foil or parchment.

While the pastry is baking, melt half the butter in a saucepan and sauté the leeks and onions over a high heat until soft and slightly browned. Add the ramsons and sauté them. Add the nettles and remaining butter with a tablespoon or two of water, cover and allow to the nettles to wilt for 2 minutes. Remove from the heat and stir all the ingredients together.

Sprinkle half of the cheese over the base of the pastry case, then add the vegetables in an even layer, and finish with the remaining cheese. Whisk the crème fraîche and milk into the eggs with some salt and pepper and the tarragon, and pour over the ingredients in the flan dish. Place in the centre of the oven straight away and bake for 25 minutes.

Serve hot or cold with salad and potatoes.

Cream of nettle soup

Serves 4

150g (5¼oz) nettles, dark stalks removed

5 chopped fresh ramsons leaves

2 tbsp olive oil

1 medium onion, diced

1 leek, cut into 1cm (⅜") rounds

1l (1¾ pints / 35fl oz) vegetable stock

1 large potato, peeled and diced

70ml (2½fl oz) double cream

Salt and pepper

Stick blender or liquidiser

Heat the oil in a deep saucepan over a medium heat. Add the onion and leek and fry for 5 minutes until soft. Add the stock and potatoes and bring up to the boil. Once boiling, reduce the heat, cover the pan and simmer for 10 minutes.

Check the potatoes are soft, if not continue simmering for another few minutes. Add the nettles and ramsons, replace the lid and allow the leaves to wilt into the soup. This will take about 2 minutes. Remove the pan from the heat and allow to stand for 5 minutes.

Using a stick blender or liquidiser, blend the soup until smooth. Stir in the cream and taste the soup, then season accordingly. Return to a medium heat until it almost boils, remove from the heat and serve.

Try making a nettle pesto with ramsons, which can be added to pasta or stews. Blend together nettles, ramsons, hazelnuts or cashews, salt and olive oil to form a paste. Transfer to a sterilised jar and seal with a layer of oil. It will keep in the fridge for about 2 weeks or can be frozen in a plastic storage container.

Summer

American elder
(*Sambucus canadensis*)

This elder is a shrub rather than a tree, reaching about 2.5m (8') high, and slowly suckering and spreading. It flowers later than the common European elder (*Sambucus nigra*), from July to November. The long flowering season and high-quality, extra-large flowers make this a valuable and easily harvested flower crop.

The flowers are harvested when fully out, preferably in dry weather. They should be picked with a minimum of green stalk and/or de-stalked afterwards.

The flavour and fragrance is not identical to common elder, but some think it is nicer, with more of a vanilla fragrance. The flowers can be used in exactly the same ways, for example as fritters – use the day lily fritters recipe in this book (see page 120) to make a light batter, and after cooking dip the fritters in caster sugar for a sweet treat. The tiny flowers that make up the umbellate head can be shaken into salads or on to cakes to add delicate flavour and decoration. But elderflowers are at their most versatile and long-lasting when made into a cordial or syrup. Once preserved in liquid form they can be added to many different drinks and puddings, including the jelly and custard recipes given here.

American elderflower cordial

Makes approximately 2l (3½ pints / 70fl oz)

20-30 heads of American elderflowers
1kg (2lb 3oz) white granulated sugar
1.5l (2¾ pints / 55fl oz) water
1 lemon, juice and zest, plus more lemon juice to taste

Muslin and sterilised glass bottles

Place the sugar into a large saucepan and add the water. Bring to the boil over a medium heat, stirring continuously until all of the sugar has dissolved. Remove from the heat and allow to cool. Once cooled, transfer to storage container with a lid.

Give the flowerheads a shake and check there are no tiny bugs hiding beneath the flowers. Put as many as can be submerged beneath the syrup into the container and add the lemon juice and zest. Stir well, replace the lid and leave in a cool place to steep for 48 hours.

Strain the liquid through muslin and discard the flowerheads. Taste a little cordial diluted in water and decide whether you would like to add more lemon juice. If so, add 1 teaspoon at a time, to taste. Pour the undiluted cordial into the bottles, screw the lids on tightly and label with the date.

Store the bottles in a cool, dark place for up to 3 months. Once opened the cordial will keep in the fridge for a month.

American elderflower jelly

Serves 4-6

75ml (2½fl oz) elderflower cordial
570ml (1 pint / 20fl oz) water
Gelatine leaves (follow instructions on packet)

Jelly mould or dessert glasses

Mix the cordial and water together in a jug. Place the gelatine leaves into a bowl and pour over enough cordial mix from the jug to just cover the leaves. Allow to soak for 10 minutes.

Add the contents of the jug and the bowl to a bain-marie – a heat-proof glass bowl set on top of a saucepan of gently simmering water. Stir until all of the gelatine has dissolved, then remove from the heat. Pour the liquid into the jelly mould or glasses and allow to cool. Once at room temperature, transfer to the fridge for at least 1 hour for the jelly to fully set.

To remove jelly from a mould, set it in warm water, just up to the rim of the mould, for 1 minute. Then place a plate on top and – holding the base firmly – flip it over and remove the mould. If the jelly is stuck, place the mould back in the warm water for a little longer, but take care not to melt it too much.

Try this with other cordials such as rose petal, or rosehip syrup, or with fruit juice. You can also add liqueurs and spirits in small quantities – make the jelly taste a little stronger than for a drink. Ensure you have the right quantity of gelatine leaves for the volume of liquid.

You can add berries and flower petals to the jelly: they will usually float upwards as it sets, which means they will be on the bottom of the jelly if using a mould.

Baked American elderflower custard with flowering quince compote

Serves 4

Compote:

300g (10½oz) flowering quinces (japonicas), quartered and de-seeded

100ml (3½fl oz) American elderflower cordial

100ml (3½fl oz) water

3 tbsp sugar (or to taste)

Custard:

100ml (3½fl oz) American elderflower cordial

480ml (16fl oz) whole milk

40g (1½oz) caster sugar

3 eggs, beaten

4 heatproof ramekin dishes

Preheat the oven to 180°C (350°F / Gas Mark 4)

Place the quartered quinces into a saucepan with the cordial, water and sugar. Bring to the boil over a medium heat and reduce to a low simmer. Cook for 5-10 minutes, stirring occasionally, until the fruit has pulped. Remove from the heat and strain through a sieve into a bowl. Spoon the purée equally between the four ramekin dishes and put to one side. For more tips on flowering quince preparation, see Flowering quince and haw chutney (Part 1, page 23).

Put the milk and cordial together in a saucepan and warm over a medium heat until almost boiling. Beat the caster sugar into the eggs and then slowly add the hot milk, stirring continuously. Pour the liquid custard into the ramekins, covering the compote and leaving 1cm (⅜") from the top of the dishes.

Set the ramekins in a deep baking tray and pour in 2.5cm (1") hot water into the tray around them. Place the baking tray in the centre of the oven and bake for 25-30 minutes. The tops will rise slightly and then sink again as they cool. Remove from the oven and serve either hot or cold as a delicious dessert.

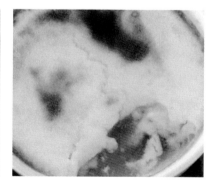

Cardoon (*Cynara cardunculus*)

Cardoon and the closely related globe artichoke are unmistakable garden plants. They come from the Mediterranean and like sun and well-drained conditions – constant winter wet is their worst enemy. Cardoons have smaller flower buds and prickly leaves, and the main crop is the thick leaf stalks. There are named varieties bred for leaf stem production.

The unprepared stalks are quite tough and woody, although they can be blanched for a few weeks to make them more tender – either covered in spring or bundled and wrapped in summer. The long, stringy fibres should be peeled, either with a vegetable peeler or by pulling the strings out with your fingers. The stems will 'bruise' when the skin is broken: rub them with lemon or submerge in lemon and water to keep them green. They then need to be boiled for 30-40 minutes, so will usually need to be pre-cooked before being added to a dish. Once prepared, cardoon has a firm and juicy texture with a mild, bittersweet taste, which works well with earthy or mild flavours such as sweet Moroccan spices or eggs.

Cardoon stems are a popular vegetable in mainland Europe and Northern Africa, particularly in Italy and Morocco. 'Carduni fritti' (see page 114) is a favourite national dish in Italy. The stem is similar to giant butterbur or oversized celery and is cooked as a vegetable or in stews. Cardoon contains useful amounts of vitamins A and C, iron, phosphorus and calcium.

Cardoon & lamb tagine

Serves 4

200g (7oz) cardoons, peeled and chopped into 2.5cm (1") lengths

2 tbsp olive oil

1 medium onion, chopped

500g (1lb 1¾oz) diced lamb

1 tsp ground turmeric

1 tbsp plain flour

500ml (18fl oz) lamb or chicken stock

1 red pepper, chopped

30g (1oz) whole pitted black olives (brined)

3 garlic cloves, crushed

2 tbsp chopped fresh coriander

2 tbsp chopped fresh fennel leaf

1 tbsp fresh ginger, peeled and finely grated

3 tsp honey

1 tsp salt

½ tsp ground cinnamon

½ tsp ground black pepper

Cast-iron casserole dish

Preheat the oven to 150°C (300°F / Gas Mark 2), or preheat a slow cooker according to the manufacturer's instructions.

Heat the olive oil in a cast-iron casserole dish or (if using a slow cooker) a large saucepan, and fry the onions on a medium heat until they begin to soften. Add the lamb and turn the heat up a little, searing the meat on all sides. Reduce the heat and add the turmeric and flour, coating the lamb pieces and onions. Pour over the stock, add all the other ingredients and stir well. If using a slow cooker, transfer the ingredients to the ceramic dish. There should be about 1cm (⅜") of stock above the other ingredients to prevent any pieces from drying out, but at least 1.5cm (⅝") between the liquid and the rim of the dish. Replace the lid and cook as follows:

Slow cooker: 8-10 hours on low. Check after 8 hours (be careful of steam as you remove the lid).

Oven: 1.5 hours, checking after 1 hour 20 minutes.

When checking the tagine, take out a piece of lamb and a piece of cardoon and allow to cool on a cold plate. Once cooled a little, see if you can cut them in half with the side of a fork. If you can, taste and see if you think they are tender enough (this is also a good time to add extra seasoning if required). If so, you can serve straight away or keep it warm until you are ready. If the lamb needs longer, keep cooking and check it again in 30 minutes.

Serve with couscous or Moroccan flatbread.

This is a great dish to serve at a dinner party and can be accompanied by other Moroccan treats such as houmous, baba ganoush, mallow leaf dolmades (see page 128) and plantain & broad bean tabbouleh (see page 133). An exotic forest garden feast!

Breaded cardoons (Carduni fritti)

Serves 4

200g (7oz) cardoons, peeled and chopped into 5cm (2") lengths

1 tbsp lemon juice

50g (1¾oz) plain flour, sifted and seasoned

2 eggs, beaten

50g (1¾oz) breadcrumbs, made from fresh or stale bread

Vegetable oil

Place the cardoons into a saucepan of boiling water with the lemon juice and boil for 30-40 minutes, until tender. Strain off the water and allow to cool.

Place the flour, eggs and breadcrumbs into three separate bowls. Taking a few at a time, place the cardoons into the flour, then into the egg, then into the breadcrumbs, ensuring that the pieces are thoroughly coated at each stage. Place the breaded cardoons carefully on to a plate, not on top of one another, ready to fry.

Fill a heavy-based saucepan or frying pan with 2.5cm (1") of vegetable oil and place over a medium heat. Test the heat occasionally by dropping in a breadcrumb. When the breadcrumbs begin to fizz the temperature is right. Reduce the heat a little to maintain the temperature and don't allow the oil to get too hot.

Add the breaded cardoons to the oil, a few at a time. Don't overcrowd the pan so you have space to turn them. When they are evenly brown and crispy all over, remove from the pan and place on to 2 sheets of kitchen paper to soak up excess oil. Fry in batches if necessary and keep them warm in the oven, or on a pre-warmed plate.

Serve as a side vegetable or as a starter with a blue cheese dipping sauce.

Chicory *(Cichorium intybus)*

Many forms of chicory are hardy perennial plants, very deep-rooted, and often used as a pasture herb and green manure in farming. The leaves of the more perennial forms can be harvested from spring to autumn. Chicory plants resemble lettuces and do not always form tight heads. The leaf colour varies from green to red in different varieties, and the leaves are often slightly bitter, especially as plants flower in the summer. Plants can be blanched for a few weeks in spring to produce leaves that are more tender. 'Witloof chicory' or chicons are the young blanched shoots of specific varieties whose roots are dug and 'forced' indoors before being discarded.

In cooking, the bitterness can be removed by wilting leaves over a flame for a few seconds. Chicory can be eaten raw as a salad leaf, or steamed, roasted or added to cooked dishes as a green. It is often used as a 'head', which is then halved or quartered before being cooked, but when growing it as a perennial it will produce for longer if leaves are picked individually. The following recipes use individual leaves, but would also work well with quartered heads of chicory.

Chicory leaves are particularly high in vitamins A and K as well as in folate, copper and manganese.

Grilled chicory with bacon & Gruyère

Serves 4

300g (10½oz) chicory leaves
4 rashers smoked streaky bacon
200ml (7fl oz) double cream
1 tsp wholegrain mustard
1 tsp fresh or dried thyme leaves
Vegetable oil
Salt and pepper
100g (3½oz) Gruyère cheese

Wash and trim the chicory leaves and place in a steamer, taking care to keep the leaves as flat as possible. Steam for 3-4 minutes, until the leaves are dark and glossy but have not completely wilted. In a square baking dish lay out the overlapping chicory leaves, as pictured, with the stalks to the centre.

Chop the bacon into 1cm (⅜") pieces and fry in a little oil until lightly browned and beginning to crisp. Remove from the heat and sprinkle over the chicory leaves.

In a small saucepan stir together the cream, mustard, half a teaspoon of thyme and seasoning. Heat gently until it begins to steam, remove from the heat and pour over the chicory and bacon. Slice the Gruyère cheese into small, thin pieces and sprinkle them on top of the cream sauce. Sprinkle on the remaining thyme and a twist of black pepper, then place under a medium grill for 10 minutes, or until the cheese begins to bubble and brown.

Cut into square portions and serve with smoked fish or baked chicken with potatoes.

Chicory, pear & hazelnut salad with blue cheese dressing

Serves 4

100g (3½oz) chicory leaves
1 iceberg lettuce
2 medium pears, cored and quartered
80g (2¾oz) whole hazelnuts

Dressing:
75ml (2½fl oz) mayonnaise
75ml (2½fl oz) soured cream
1 tsp Dijon mustard
Salt and pepper
30g (1oz) blue cheese

Garnish:
Pear, cut into segments
Hazelnuts

Coarsely chop half the lettuce and all of the chicory leaves and add to a salad bowl. Cut the remaining lettuce half into 4 segments and arrange in a cross shape on to a plate with the bases meeting in the middle and the cut edges all facing the same direction. Pile the chopped leaves on to the centre of the plate.

Cut one pear quarter into long, thin segments and put to one side. Dice the remaining pear quarters and scatter over the salad, along with the hazelnuts.

For the dressing, combine the mayonnaise and soured cream in a dish and stir in the mustard, salt and pepper. Crumble in the blue cheese and stir in well. Spoon the dressing on to the centre of the salad and garnish with the strips of pear and a few hazelnuts.

Alternatively you can coarsely chop the leaves, dice the pears and toss all together with the hazelnuts and serve ready dressed.

Day lilies (*Hemerocallis* spp.)

There are several species and hundreds of varieties of *Hemerocallis* – grassy-leaved plants that grow in any soil or situation. Day lilies are widely used as garden flowering plants, and the large bright flowers are a fine vegetable crop, containing useful quantities of vitamin C, potassium and phosphorus. Unlike most edible flowers, they are really substantial: thick-petalled and crunchy, with a delightfully perfumed and mildly peppery flavour, which can be used in soups, salads and vegetable dishes. In the light summery soup shown opposite, the aromatic flavour of the day lilies beautifully complements the subtle sweetness of the courgettes.

The bright peach-orange colour of the flowers makes them decorative as well as tasty, and when cooked they add a subtle yellow tinge to the dish they are added to. They can also be enjoyed as a side dish, sautéd in a little butter or fried in a light crispy batter. The older flowers that are beginning to wilt are said to have the strongest flavour, but the unopened buds and fresh, opened flowers hold their shape better if being used whole. The unopened flower buds taste rather like green beans.

Harvest flower buds early in the morning before they open, and flowers towards the end of the day. The previous day's withered flowers can also be picked and dried for seasoning.

Day lily & courgette soup

Serves 4

80g (2¾oz) day lily flowers, finely chopped

30g (1oz) butter

1 tbsp olive oil

1 medium onion, finely chopped

2 celery sticks, chopped

300g (10½oz) courgettes, diced

2 garlic cloves, crushed

200g (7oz) potatoes, diced

1l (1¾ pints / 35fl oz) vegetable stock

Salt and pepper

Garnish:

Crème fraîche or yogurt

Stick blender

Before chopping the day lilies you can clean them using a dry pastry brush. Avoid using water, as this washes away some of the pollen, which gives them much of their flavour and colour.

Melt the butter in a large saucepan over a low heat and combine with the olive oil. Add the onion, celery and courgettes and fry over a medium heat for about 3 minutes until soft. Add the garlic and fry for a further 2 minutes. Add the potatoes and stock, cover the pan and bring to the boil. Reduce to a simmer and cook for 10 minutes.

Add the day lilies and cook for a further 5 minutes. Remove from the heat and blend until smooth, using a stick blender. Season to taste and return to heat. Bring the soup just up to boiling, remove from the heat and serve.

Serve with a little crème fraîche or yogurt.

Day lily fritters

Serves 4

12 whole day lily flowers or buds
50g (1¾oz) plain flour, sifted
¼ tsp ground ginger
¼ tsp bicarbonate of soda
Pinch of salt
150ml (5¼fl oz) sparkling water
Vegetable oil

Clean the flowerheads by brushing with a dry pastry brush, taking care not to remove too much of the pollen. Try not to crush the flowers as you handle them, so they will keep their shape when battered.

In a mixing bowl combine the flour, ginger, bicarbonate of soda and salt. Gradually whisk in the sparkling water until you have a smooth batter.

Take a heavy-based saucepan and fill with 2.5-5cm (1-2") of vegetable oil. Place over a medium heat and test occasionally by dropping in a little batter. When the batter effervesces in the oil, the temperature is right. Reduce the heat a little to maintain the temperature and don't allow the oil to get too hot.

One by one, dip each flowerhead into the batter and drop into the hot oil. Do not overcrowd the pan so you can see each fritter and turn if needed to achieve a uniform colour. When the fritters are golden-brown and crisp, remove them from the oil and place on to kitchen paper. Transfer to a clean plate and serve with a simple fresh dip, such as plain yogurt or crème fraîche. The delicate flavour of the fritters will be lost if eaten with a dipping sauce which is too strong in

flavour. They are deliciously moreish, so if you have plenty of day lilies in flower you may want to double the quantities in this recipe!

Try this fritter recipe with American elderflowers. After frying, dip the fritters into fine caster sugar and serve with vanilla ice cream and raspberries for a delicious summer dessert.

The dried flowerbuds are known in China as 'golden needles' and are much used in cooking, usually soaked in water for 30 minutes to reconstitute them before adding to recipes. They can be chopped into salads, or cooked by steaming, frying, etc. In soups and stews they are used also for their thickening effect.

Elephant garlic
(*Allium ampeloprasum* var. *ampeloprasum*)

In reality a kind of perennial leek, elephant garlic has been grown since ancient times. In winter and spring it looks much like a leek, and then in summer it puts up a tall flowering head up to 1.5m (5') high, with pinky-blue flowers in a round head. The bulbs, which are harvested after flowering, look like giant garlic: each one up to 10cm (4") across, subdivided into giant cloves.

The flavour is like mild garlic and the cloves can be used in the same ways as garlic, though being both bigger and milder they can also be treated more like a vegetable rather than as a spice or flavouring. They are particularly good when roasted, becoming soft and sweet, and working well in combination with starchy root vegetables and squashes in the autumn and winter.

Like garlic, elephant garlic contains antioxidants and antibiotic compounds. The young leaves are also edible, with a leek–garlic flavour.

Baked elephant garlic & Camembert

This recipe is the ultimate dinner-party starter to share. Baked whole in its skin, the elephant garlic can be spread on to French toast and dipped into the wonderful gooey Camembert infused with rosemary, thyme and a little more garlic! The quality of garlic when roasted is a sweet, spread-able paste with a mild and mellow flavour, which is perfectly complemented by the earthy, creamy baked cheese.

Serves 4-6

Baked garlic:

1 whole bulb elephant garlic

Olive oil

Baked Camembert:

1 whole Camembert cheese

1 elephant garlic clove, finely sliced

A few sprigs of fresh rosemary and thyme

1 white baguette, sliced into small rounds and lightly buttered on each side

Preheat the oven to 180°C (350°F / Gas Mark 4)

Begin by peeling off the outer layers of skin from the garlic bulb, leaving the skin of the cloves intact. Slice off just the first 1cm (⅜") from the tops of the cloves, to expose the flesh. Set the bulb on a sheet of foil on top of a baking tray and scrunch up the sides of the foil a little to form a bowl. Drizzle olive oil over the whole bulb and then draw up the sides of the foil and join at the top to wrap it loosely. Place in the top of the oven and bake for between 1 hour and 1 hour 30 minutes. The cooking time will vary significantly depending on the size of the bulb, so check it after 1 hour by piercing the largest clove with a knife. The clove should be totally soft and golden brown, and will have shrunk away from the skins when ready.

While the garlic is cooking, remove the Camembert from its wrapping. If it has come in a wooden box you can return the unwrapped cheese to the bottom half of the box, otherwise transfer it to a shallow, ovenproof dish that it can fit into fairly snugly. You can add a layer of baking parchment beneath the cheese to prevent it sticking on to the dish – this also makes it easier to get the last morsels of cheese out when eating.

Pierce the top of the cheese in a few places and insert the finely sliced garlic and sprigs of herbs. Place the dish in the centre of a large baking tray with the baguette slices around it. When the garlic is almost cooked, place the tray in the centre of the oven and bake for 15-20 minutes. Keep an eye on the baguette slices and remove them when they are golden brown.

Remove everything from the oven and arrange on to a wooden board. With a sharp knife cut a cross shape into the top of the Camembert and peel back the rind. You may decide to break up the garlic bulb to make it easier to get the flesh out of the skins, but it does look good when presented whole. Place the cheese in the centre of the table and guests can take pieces of toast, spread them with the baked garlic and dip them into the cheese – a very simple, rustic fondue!

Other recipes using elephant garlic: Brined elephant garlic (Part 1, page 49).

Roasted elephant garlic & beetroot with feta & rosemary

Serves 4

8 elephant garlic cloves, peeled or left in skins

3 medium beetroot, cut into wedges

85ml (3fl oz) olive oil

2 sprigs of fresh rosemary, leaves stripped from stalks

Salt and coarsely ground black pepper

150g (5¼oz) feta cheese, crumbled

Preheat the oven to 180°C (350°F / Gas Mark 4)

Place the garlic and beetroot into a deep roasting pan. Pour in the olive oil and toss until the vegetables are completely covered. Sprinkle over the rosemary leaves, salt and pepper.

Place in the top of the oven and roast for 30-40 minutes, or until soft in the middle and crispy on the outside.

Turn off the oven, remove the baking tray and transfer the beetroot and garlic to an ovenproof vegetable dish. Sprinkle with the feta cheese and return to the cooling oven for another 10 minutes. This allows the feta to soften and dry a little, which improves the texture.

Remove from the oven and serve. This is particularly good with roast lamb.

Limes (*Tilia* spp.)

Also known as lindens

Lime leaves are a real seasonal treat from the forest garden. As a raw salad leaf they fill the same niche as lettuce, being soft, mild and bulky with just enough crunch. In addition to these fine qualities they are beautiful: their colour has a luminosity that captures the essence of springtime and brightens up any salad bowl medley. But they can also be steamed like leafy greens, and a fine pesto can be made to capture them at their youthful peak.

Young leaves of all lime/linden trees can be eaten, but those from small-leaved lime (*Tilia cordata*) are often favourites, with a lovely texture and colour. To grow lime leaves seriously as a vegetable, you need to coppice or pollard the trees to keep them bushy.

Lime leaves can be harvested from the tree shoot tips through most of the growing season.

Lime leaf salad

Serves 4

200g (7oz) fresh lime leaves
1 eating apple, diced
2 celery sticks, chopped
2 tbsp raisins
Handful of croutons
30g (1oz) mature cheddar

Dressing:
4 tbsp mayonnaise
Half a lemon, juice and zest
3 tbsp chopped fresh coriander leaves

Rinse and dry the lime leaves and arrange in the bottom and around the sides of a salad bowl. Add the apple and celery to the bowl. Sprinkle the raisins and croutons over the salad, then crumble, grate or shave the cheddar (depending on the texture) on top.

Combine the dressing ingredients in a separate bowl and then spoon over the salad or serve on the side.

Lime leaf pesto

As with some other pesto recipes included in these pages, quantities are approximate and ratios are variable depending on what you have available and what you like. This a just an example of one combination of ingredients, but essentially you need leaves, oil, nuts, garlic and a little salt – cheese is optional – to make a pesto. Always use clean, preferably sterilised jars, and seal the paste with a little extra oil before replacing the lid. Fresh pesto will keep for 2 weeks in the fridge, or up to 3 months in the freezer.

Handful of lime leaves
4 tbsp olive oil
2 tbsp raw peanuts
Sprig of fresh basil and/or oregano
2 garlic cloves
½ tsp salt

Optional:
30g (1oz) Parmesan

Food processor or stick blender

Rinse and dry the lime leaves and place all the ingredients in a food processor. Blend to form a paste, adding more oil if necessary. You can also use a stick blender, although more oil is needed to achieve a smooth consistency. Taste and tweak as required.

Transfer to jars or freezer containers, label and seal.

Mallows (*Malva* spp.)

The leaves of all the *Malva* mallow species, both annual and perennial, are edible. The Chinese mallow (*M. verticillata*), pictured here, is commonly grown as a vegetable in China. Mallow grows wild in Turkey, Morocco and other Middle Eastern regions, and is eaten there as a nutritious leaf vegetable.

Two of the nicest perennial mallows to eat are musk mallow (*M. moschata*) and wood mallow (*M. sylvestris*), both of which are native to the UK.

The younger leaves are always more tender and are more suitable for salads. Flowers can also be added to salads. The more delicate varieties of mallow are good raw in salads, but the larger leaves can be a little thick and fuzzy, and are better cooked. Mallow leaves have a thickening quality when cooked, which makes them a useful addition to green soups and stews. Later in the season the seed heads, known as 'cheeses' due to their wheel-like shape, can be picked and eaten straight off the plant, or tossed in salads.

Mallow leaf dolmades

We tend to think of this popular Middle Eastern snack as stuffed vine leaves, but it is not unusual to find them made locally with mallow leaves.

Makes 16

16 large mallow leaves

Half an onion, grated

4 tbsp olive oil

100g (3½oz) risotto rice

4 tbsp lemon juice

3 tbsp chopped fresh mint

3 tbsp chopped fresh fennel leaf

Salt and pepper

Wash and dry the mallow leaves and chop off the stalks just above where the leaf ribs converge, so the leaves lie completely flat. Blanch them in boiling water for 1 minute to soften them, then lay them out on kitchen paper or a clean tea towel.

Fry the onion in 2 tablespoons of olive oil over a medium heat for 3 minutes. Add the rice, 2 table-spoons of lemon juice, 2 tablespoons of water, herbs and plenty of salt and pepper. Stir the ingredients together, making sure the rice is fully coated with liquid, and cook for 2 minutes on a low heat.

Place 1 heaped tablespoon of the rice mixture in the centre of each mallow leaf. Transfer to a flat surface and mould the rice into a sausage shape parallel to and to one side of the midrib of each leaf. Fold the base edge of the leaf first, then the top, then one side. Finally, remould the rice beneath the leaf into a tight sausage and roll from the folded side over the remaining flap of leaf to form a long parcel. The moisture in the leaves will help the flaps stick together.

Place the dolmades into the base of a saucepan. You can add a second layer by putting a layer of leaves on top of the first dolmades, then arranging the next layer on top. Pour the remaining olive oil and lemon juice over the dolmades and add 200ml (7fl oz) of cold water to the saucepan. Put a smaller pan lid or heavy plate on top of the dolmades and cover the pan.

Bring to the boil on a medium heat and then turn down low and simmer for 25 minutes. The dolmades will gently steam until the water has been absorbed, leaving only the oil in the bottom of the pan. Check occasionally and add a little more water if needed. When the dolmades are ready, the rice should be soft enough for a fork to sink into them easily. Lay them out on to kitchen paper to cool. They will keep in the fridge for a week.

Other recipes using mallows: Ice plant with peanuts and coconut (page 86).

Mountain sorrel
(*Oxyria digyna*)

This sorrel is a small plant, growing 30-40cm (1'-1'4") high, and likes a well-drained site. It produces many flattish, winged seeds which can spread about easily, so is liable to self-seed.

The leaves have a lovely succulent texture and lemony flavour. Like other sorrels, it has a strong, tangy lemon flavour and is great added raw to salads or cooked in soups and sauces. The citrus tang works very well with fish, particularly strongly flavoured, oily fish such as salmon or mackerel. It also works well with eggs and is delicious added to omelettes, or wilted under a poached egg on toast.

The leaves can be harvested right through the growing season, but are nicest in the spring.

Pan-fried salmon fillet & scallops with a mountain sorrel sauce

The fresh tang of sorrel leaves balances the richness of the salmon and scallops in this indulgent dish.

Serves 4

Sauce:
Handful of mountain sorrel leaves, finely shredded
30g (1oz) butter
22g (¾oz) flour
400ml (14fl oz) milk
2 tbsp chopped fresh parsley
2 tbsp chopped fresh chives
Salt and pepper

30g (1oz) butter
4 salmon fillets
20 scallops
1 tsp balsamic vinegar

Garnish:
Raw, shredded sorrel leaves

Rinse the salmon and scallops and pat them dry.

Melt the butter (for the sauce) in a small saucepan and remove from the heat. Add the flour to make a roux, and gradually stir in the cold milk. Add the mountain sorrel, herbs and seasoning and return to a medium heat. Gently bring the sauce to the boil, stirring all the time, and then reduce to a very low heat while you cook the fish, remembering to stir occasionally.

Melt half of the remaining butter in a large frying pan over a medium heat. Place in the salmon fillets and fry on both sides until browned. Cooking time will vary depending on the size and thickness of the fillets. Check your thickest fillet by pushing a knife in between the flakes of flesh to see the colour within. The centre should still have some rosiness to it, but be hot and firm.

When the salmon is cooked, place the fillets on to a preheated plate and keep warm in the oven while you cook the scallops. Add the remaining butter to the frying pan and add the scallops. Fry them for 2-3 minutes on each side – again, the cooking time will depend on the size of the scallops. Add the balsamic vinegar and cook for another 1-2 minutes on each side until they have browned around the edges.

Serve the fish on a bed of steamed sea beet or chard with the sauce poured over it and garnish with raw, shredded sorrel leaves.

Other recipes using mountain sorrel: Sea beet with toasted seeds (page 136).

Plantains (*Plantago* spp.)

Plantain leaves need to be young and eaten fresh to avoid disappointment. In dry spells the leaves can sometimes be a little tough. Buck's horn plantain (*P. coronopis*) and ribwort plantain (*P. lanceolata*) are often considered to be the best; both bear long, narrow leaves that stay tender most of the season. These grow as lettuce-sized plants in most soils but produce the best leaves in a moist soil that does not dry out too much.

Plantains are high in minerals, notably potassium and phosphorus, and are valued as pasture herbs for that reason.

The leaves are mainly harvested through the spring, but new tender leaves can also be produced later in the summer after flowering. Very dry weather can make leaves tougher, and the best-quality leaves are harvested from plants specifically grown with little competition, rather than plants in pastures, which are more prone to drought stress.

Plantain & broad bean tabbouleh

Tabbouleh is an Arabian salad made with bulgur wheat, tomatoes, mint and other fresh herbs. It requires plenty of green, herby bulk to balance the bulgur wheat, and plantain grows very vigorously so is ideal for the purpose. Plantain leaves have a soft, herb-like flavour and thick, ribbed leaves, so they work very well finely chopped into salads or added to green soups.

30g (1oz) plantain leaves, finely chopped
200g (7oz) bulgur wheat
200g (7oz) fresh broad beans, podded
3 tbsp olive oil
1 tbsp lemon juice
6 sun-dried tomato halves, finely chopped

Half a red pepper, finely chopped
3 welsh onion leaves or spring onions, finely chopped
1 tbsp finely chopped fresh mint
1 tbsp finely chopped fennel leaf

Cook the bulgur wheat according to the instructions on the packet. Strain and put aside to cool. Steam the broad beans for 4 minutes and put aside to cool.

In a small jug, combine the oil and lemon juice, then pour over the bulgar wheat. Add all the other ingredients to the cooled bulgur wheat and mix thoroughly.

Serve cold as part of a mezze or buffet.

Plantain & sweet cicely soup

Serves 4

80g (2¾oz) plantain leaves, roughly chopped
Vegetable oil
1 onion, diced
3 garlic cloves, crushed
500g (1lb 1¾oz) potato, diced
1.2l (2 pints / 40fl oz) vegetable stock
Small handful of sweet cicely leaves, roughly chopped

Garnish:
Croutons or toasted pumpkin seeds
Crème fraîche or soured cream

Stick blender or liquidiser

Heat a little oil in a deep saucepan and fry the onion on a medium heat for 5 minutes. Add the garlic and fry for a further 2 minutes. Add the potatoes and stock to the saucepan and bring to the boil. Reduce to a medium heat and simmer for 8 minutes.

Add the plantain and sweet cicely to the saucepan and simmer for another 8 minutes.

Remove from the heat and blend the soup using a stick blender or liquidiser. Season to taste and return to the heat. Turn off the heat when it begins to boil and serve with croutons or toasted pumpkin seeds sprinkled on top. Try stirring in a spoonful of crème fraîche or soured cream for extra richness.

Tender plantain leaves are also an excellent salad ingredient: the mucilaginous leaves add a nice texture.

Sea beet (*Beta vulgaris maritima*)

Sea beet is the wild ancestor of beetroot and Swiss chard. It grows wild around the coast but can be cultivated in any well-drained soil, making bushy plants that can reach 1m (3') high when they flower in summer.

Sea beet is a mild, leafy green; a versatile vegetable that fulfils the role of spinach or chard when added to dishes or cooked as a side vegetable. The leaves have a wonderful deep green colour. It doesn't shrink quite as much as spinach when cooked, and in texture is more comparable to chard. The recipes given here are some simple ideas for side dishes, but sea beet is also great in green soups, quiches, stir-fries and with seafood.

The leaves are likely to have similar or higher nutritional levels than ordinary beetroot leaves. The latter are very high in vitamins A, B, C, E and K, and also in many minerals.

Sea beet leaves can be harvested right through the growing season, and even in winter in mild locations.

Creamed sea beet with toasted almonds

Serves 4

400g (14oz) sea beet leaves, finely shredded
1 large onion, finely chopped
3 garlic cloves, finely chopped
30g (1oz) butter
½ tsp ground nutmeg
Salt and pepper
340ml (12fl oz) double cream
30g (1oz) whole almonds

Melt the butter in a saucepan, add the onion and garlic and fry over a medium heat until the onion becomes translucent. Add the sea beet to the pan. Cover and allow it to wilt for 3 minutes, stirring occasionally.

Stir in the nutmeg, seasoning and cream and bring to just before boiling point. In a heavy-based saucepan, gently toast the almonds until they begin to brown, and then remove from the heat. Serve the creamed sea beet with the toasted almonds scattered on top.

Sea beet with toasted seeds

Serves 4

400g (14oz) sea beet leaves, finely shredded
Handful of mountain sorrel, finely shredded
3 tbsp pumpkin seeds
2 tsp cumin seeds
2 tsp mustard seeds
Sunflower oil
1 large red onion, finely sliced
4 tbsp chopped fresh coriander
Salt and pepper

Add the seeds to a large heavy-based frying pan and toast on a low heat for 2 minutes, until they begin to release their aroma and brown a little. The mustard seeds will begin to 'pop' when they are ready. Remove from the heat and put the seeds in a bowl to one side.

Heat a little sunflower oil in the frying pan and fry the red onion on a medium heat for 3 minutes, until it becomes translucent. Add the sea beet and sorrel, turn to a low heat and cover for 2 minutes. Remove the lid and stir in the toasted seeds and seasoning. Turn up to a high heat and stir-fry for a further 2 minutes. Serve piping hot with meat, fish or eggs.

Snowbell tree (*Halesia carolina*)

Sometimes grown as an ornamental slow-growing small garden tree, the snowbell tree has pretty white flowers in spring, followed by interestingly shaped green fruits that are nice as a vegetable. They have a lovely cucumber / green pea flavour and a fine crunchy texture. After good flowering weather in April, masses of fruits can set.

The young green four-winged fruits are harvested as they get to full size in July for about 3 weeks, after which they get too tough to use.

Prepare the fruits by simply trimming off stalks and add them raw to salads, or lightly cooked as a side vegetable. They work well in stir-fries and other vegetable dishes, where their fresh, delicate flavour won't be smothered, or their crisp texture lost.

Snowbell fruits with courgette & fennel

Serves 4

400g (14oz) snowbell tree fruits, trimmed

30g (1oz) butter

2 tbsp olive oil

200g (7oz) courgettes, halved lengthways and thinly sliced

1 medium fennel bulb, finely sliced

2 garlic cloves, finely chopped

4 welsh onion leaves, finely chopped

1 tbsp chopped fresh mint

Melt the butter with the olive oil in a wok or large frying pan and heat until the butter begins to bubble. Add the snowbell fruits, courgettes and fennel to the wok and stir-fry on a medium-high heat for 5 minutes. Add the garlic and fry for a further 3 minutes until the vegetables begin to brown slightly but still have some crunch. Finally, stir in the herbs and remove from the heat.

Serve straight from the wok as an accompaniment to meat or fish.

Try this with some nuts and seeds thrown in and serve with egg-fried rice and a dash of soy sauce as a vegetarian main course.

You can also treat the green fruits like mange-tout peas and put them in stir-fries, salads, etc.

Other recipes using snowbell fruits: Snowbell pickles (Part 1, page 50).

Sorrels (*Rumex* spp.)

The sorrel and dock family contains many members which have edible parts; the sorrels are generally nicer than the docks, being more tender and with a finer flavour.

Garden sorrel (*R. acetosa*) is the commonly grown species, although French sorrel (*R. scutatus*) and sheep's sorrel (*R. acetosella*) are equally nice. The leaves and young stems of these are harvested through the growing season. There are also some varieties of garden sorrel that are evergreen so can be harvested in winter too. The leaves have a lemony sharpness due to oxalic acid, which is fine to eat in moderation – just don't eat sorrel soup every day! The simple sauce recipes that follow capture their flavour and can be added to dishes for a little zing.

All members of the family have deep taproots and are excellent mineral accumulators, making the leaves high in potassium, phosphorus and other minerals.

Sorrel sauce

30g (1oz) sorrel leaves
1 tbsp white sugar
1 tbsp boiling water
4 tbsp white wine vinegar
1½ tsp cornflour

Stick blender

Combine the sugar and water and stir until the sugar has dissolved. Add the white wine vinegar and sorrel leaves and blend with a stick blender until fairly smooth. It's nice to leave some 'bits' of leaf to add texture.

Combine the cornflour with 1 tablespoon of cold water and stir until the flour has dissolved. Transfer the sorrel sauce to a small saucepan and heat gently, gradually stirring in the cornflour. As the sauce heats, it will thicken; stir constantly to avoid lumps, and remove from the heat as soon as the sauce has thickened. Sadly the sauce loses its vibrant green colour when heated, but the sooner you remove it from the heat, the less brown it will become.

Transfer to a clean, dry jar and allow to cool. Refrigerate; the sauce will keep for 6 weeks.

Sorrel tartare

6 large sorrel leaves, finely chopped

2 tsp capers (brined), finely chopped

1 spring onion, finely chopped

4 tbsp mayonnaise

2 tbsp crème fraîche

1 tbsp chopped fresh parsley

Combine all the ingredients, adding a little of the brine from the capers jar, and mix well.

This sauce is delicious with all kinds of fish and will keep for around 10 days (check the date on the crème fraîche).

Sorrel leaves can be used sparingly in salads as well as in cooked dishes.

Try sorrel with poached eggs and muffins. Make a sorrel purée by wilting shredded leaves into a little butter with salt and pepper, and serve on top of a toasted English muffin, then perch a perfectly soft poached egg on top for a delicious brunch.

Other recipes using sorrels: Pan-fried sea bass with fennel & puréed sorrel (page 74).

Turkish rocket
(*Bunias orientalis*)

A deep-rooted brassica relative, Turkish rocket is a robust perennial plant that can grow about 1m (3') high when flowering in summer.

There are two main crops from Turkish rocket. One is the leaves, harvested mainly in spring. They have a mustard flavour that gets hotter as plants start to flower. Good raw in salads when very young, they are otherwise best cooked, either by themselves (as a kind of mustardy spinach) or in other dishes.

The other main crop is the unopened flowerheads, which look like those of broccoli and are used in all the same ways. Like the leaves, they too have a mustard flavour, but this is never too hot. Once the flowers come out, the flowering tips can also be used in salads.

This plant is very easy to grow in most soils and situations, even in heavy shade.

Turkish rocket & potato salad

Serves 4

30g (1oz) Turkish rocket flowerheads, roughly chopped
800g (1lb 12oz) good boiling potatoes
3 tbsp pine nuts
7g (¼oz) chopped fresh spearmint
Salt and pepper to taste
100g (3½oz) crème fraîche

Garnish:
Chopped Turkish rocket and spearmint leaves

If the potatoes have bad skins (they are likely to be old when Turkish rocket is flowering) then peel them, otherwise just scrub and chop into 2.5cm (1") cubes. Place in a saucepan, cover with boiling water and simmer for 5-8 minutes, until they drop off smoothly when you push a fork into them. It is important to ensure that the potatoes don't become too soft, as they will become mushy when mixed with the crème fraîche. Strain the potatoes, put into a mixing bowl and leave to cool.

Put aside some of the chopped rocket and spearmint to use as a garnish. Set a non-stick frying pan on a medium heat for 1 minute before adding the pine nuts. Toast for about 2 minutes, tossing occasionally until browned.

When the potatoes are fully cooled, add the pine nuts, Turkish rocket and mint – if they are still too warm they may wilt the leaves. Add salt and pepper and the crème fraîche and gently turn into the potatoes. Transfer to a serving bowl and garnish with the remaining chopped shoots and leaves.

This salad will keep well in the fridge for 3 or 4 days and goes nicely with grilled white fish.

Patrick Whitefield's summer salad

The permaculture author Patrick Whitefield has been growing perennial vegetables for many years, and each year experiments with different seasonal salads picked from his garden. One of his spring salads appears on page 72. Here is his recipe for a simple and flavoursome salad picked in August.

Bronze fennel
Musk mallow
Nasturtium leaves
Pot marigold petals
Turkish rocket

Pick the Turkish rocket, musk mallow and nasturtium leaves in equal, generous portions, then add smaller sprinklings of fennel and marigold petals.

This also works well with added winter purslane and welsh onion. If grown in the shade, welsh onion leaves will remain green and succulent in summer.

Warm Turkish rocket & lentil salad

Serves 4

70g (2½oz) Turkish rocket leaves, flowerheads and flowers, roughly chopped

200g (7oz) green, brown or puy lentils

1 medium red onion, finely chopped

2 tbsp olive oil

2 garlic cloves, finely chopped

1 tbsp finely chopped sweet cicely seeds, or 1 tsp bruised fennel seeds

4 medium fresh tomatoes, diced

2 tbsp lemon juice

1 tbsp chopped fresh mint

1 tbsp chopped fresh sweet cicely or fennel leaf

100g (3½oz) feta cheese, diced into 1cm (⅜") cubes

Salt and pepper

Garnish:

Turkish rocket flowers

Rinse and cook the lentils according to the instructions on the packet.

Fry the onion in the olive oil on a low heat for 3 minutes. Keep a few Turkish rocket flowers aside for a garnish. Add the garlic, sweet cicely seeds (or fennel seeds) and Turkish rocket to the onions and fry for a further 2 minutes. Stir in the fresh tomatoes, lemon juice and herbs and put to one side. Strain the cooked lentils, add them to the saucepan with the onions and stir together. Return to a low heat for 3 minutes, stirring continuously. Remove from the heat, add the feta cheese and fold in gently until evenly distributed. Season with salt and pepper.

Add the flowers as a garnish and serve warm with a green salad and bread.

Welsh onion *(Allium fistulosum)*

One of the more commonly grown perennial onion species, welsh onion forms a clump of bulbs as it grows, each with a number of cylindrical hollow shoots growing upwards to about 40cm (1'4") high. The name 'welsh' derives from the Old English 'welisc', meaning 'foreign', and does not refer to the country Wales!

The main crop from welsh onion is the leaves, which can be harvested several times a year, allowing plants to recover after each cut. They can be used in salads or cooked in other recipes – they don't require much cooking. The bulbs can also be used, just like shallots or small onions.

Welsh onions are high in vitamins A and C and, like all the onion family, contain compounds that are antibacterial and antifungal. They are easy to grow in most soils in a fairly sunny position.

Welsh onion & goat's cheese pancakes

Makes about six drop-scone-sized pancakes.

6 welsh onion leaves, finely chopped
150g (5¼oz) plain flour, sifted
1 tsp bicarbonate of soda
Salt and pepper
1 egg
340ml (12fl oz) cows' or goats' milk
100g (3½oz) hard goats' cheese, finely diced
Vegetable oil or butter

Combine the flour, bicarbonate of soda, salt and pepper in a mixing bowl and make a small dip in the centre. Break the egg into the dip and add a little milk. Gradually whisk the egg and milk into the surrounding flour, adding more milk as you go. Beat until you have a smooth batter, then add the cheese and welsh onion.

Melt a little oil or butter in a non-stick frying pan or griddle (flat, not ridged). When the oil is hot, ladle in enough batter to form a pancake roughly 13cm (5") in diameter. You can use the back of the ladle to smooth and shape the pancake. Fry each pancake for about 2 minutes on each side, or until it is golden brown. As each pancake is finished place it on to a plate in a warm oven to keep hot.

Serve hot with a side salad.

Other recipes using welsh onion: Plantain & broad bean tabbouleh (page 133); Crunchy yacon salad (page 223); Siberian purslane salad (page 217).

Autumn

Apple rose (*Rosa rugosa*)

Also known as rugosa rose

A very common plant in gardens and hedges in the UK, apple rose makes a bushy shrub up to 2m (6'6") high, sometimes gradually suckering and spreading to form larger colonies. It has been long naturalised and some conservationists dislike it; however, it is a valuable bee plant and its rosehips are hard to beat. The large flowers are produced from May onwards.

The rosehips on apple rose are round and very large (25-35mm/1-1⅜"), ripening from September onwards. There is a long tradition in the UK of making rosehip juices and syrups, which are exceptionally high in vitamin C. The form of vitamin C in rosehips is very resistant to breaking down at high temperatures, e.g. during cooking.

Rosehips are also high in vitamins A, E and K, as well as in many minerals.

Apple rose petal cordial

Makes approximately 2l (3½ pints)

12 apple rose flowerheads
2l (3½ pints / 70fl oz) water
2 tbsp lemon juice
255g (9oz) white granulated sugar

Glass storage jars, approx. 1.5l (2¾ pint / 55fl oz)
Muslin and sterilised bottles

Remove the petals from the flowerheads, discarding the head and any brown or shrivelled petals. You will notice that the larger petals have thick, white bases – these can have a slightly bitter flavour, so you may want to trim them with a pair of scissors.

Add the rose petals to the water and lemon juice. If you use 1.5l (2¾ pint / 55fl oz) glass storage jars, each with 1l (1¾ pints / 35fl oz) of water and the petals divided between the two, this allows plenty of space for steeping. Allow the petals to steep for 48 hours in a cool, dark place.

Strain the petal water through muslin into a saucepan, squeezing all the water from the petals. Add the sugar to the pan and bring to the boil over a medium heat, stirring occasionally. Just as it comes to the boil, turn off the heat and pour into sterilised bottles. Allow to cool.

Once opened it is best stored in the fridge and will keep for up to 2 months. Dilute to taste, approximately 1 part cordial to 10 parts water.

Try adding this cordial to lemonade or soda, to biscuit or cake mixes, or to fruity jelly. To make a delicious rose lassi (an Indian yogurt drink), add 1 part cordial to 1 part water and 3 parts plain yogurt.

Apple rose flowers are highly fragrant and make a lovely addition to summer salads.

The easiest way to process the fruits for juices, etc., is to use a steam juice extractor. This is a 3-layer pan system which sits on a cooker with boiling water beneath, a juice collector in the middle and fruit in the top layer. With rosehips you can just halve or quarter the fruit and put the whole lot in the top pan – seeds, hairs and all. After about an hour you end up with a concentrated clear juice which can be bottled as it is or sweetened first.

To preserve for herb teas or as a spice, the hips should be halved, the seeds and hairs removed with a teaspoon, and the halved 'shells' dried (in a dehydrator if necessary) before grinding to a coarse powder.

Rose creams

1 tbsp rose petal cordial
2 tbsp rosehip syrup
3 tbsp double cream
400g (14oz) icing sugar
100g (3½oz) dark cooking chocolate

Combine the cordial, cream and syrup in a mixing bowl. Sift in half the icing sugar and stir in thoroughly to form a paste. Gradually sift in the remaining icing sugar until it forms a dough which can be made into a ball. Knead the dough to ensure the ingredients are well mixed and then divide into balls about 3cm (1 ⅛") across. Flatten the balls slightly and place on a plate, then put in the fridge to harden.

Break the dark chocolate into pieces and place in a glass, heat-proof dish. Set the bowl on top of a small saucepan of boiling water to create a bain-marie. Place the pan over a low heat and stir the chocolate until it has completely melted.

Dip the rose creams into the melted chocolate, so that the sweet is half covered.

This is a great recipe to make to keep children entertained, and can be made in other flavours using peppermint syrup, elderflower cordial or rose petal cordial on its own.

Rosehip syrup

Makes approximately 1l (1¾ pints / 35fl oz)

Making a syrup concentrate from the rosehip juice is a perfect way to preserve it. It can then be used in other recipes, such as for rose creams (above).

500g (1lb 1¾oz) rosehips, de-stalked, tailed and halved
500ml (18fl oz) water
180g (6½oz) granulated sugar

Steam juice extractor
Muslin and sterilised bottle

Place the halved hips into a steam juice extractor (as described on page 149) or place the rosehips and water into a heavy-based saucepan and bring to the boil. Reduce the heat and simmer until the hips have turned to pulp. Remove from the heat and allow to cool. Strain the watery pulp through a muslin cloth, discard the seeds and pulp and return the juice to the saucepan. Add the sugar and bring to the boil again. Reduce heat and simmer for 5 minutes.

Transfer the syrup to a sterilised bottle and store in the fridge. The syrup will keep for at least 3 months.

Rosehip ripple ice cream

200g (7oz) rosehips, de-stalked and tailed

100ml (3½fl oz) water

30g (1oz) caster sugar

570ml (1 pint) double or whipping cream

1 tsp vanilla extract

1 tin (400g) condensed milk

Rosehips are full of seeds and fine fibres, which need to be removed before consumption. There are different way to do this, one of which is to halve the hips and scoop out the seeds with a teaspoon. This method is very time-consuming and you may want to sieve the pulp after cooking anyway, to ensure all the fibres are removed. Alternatively you can cook the hips, whole or halved, in water, and then sieve them to remove the seeds and fibres – this tends to leave you with a little less usable pulp per weight, but is much quicker. This is the method used in this recipe. If you choose to de-seed with a spoon you will need slightly fewer rosehips, about 170g (6oz).

Place the rosehips in a heavy-based saucepan with the water and bring to the boil. Reduce the heat and simmer for 5-10 minutes, until the hips have pulped. Remove from the heat and push through a sieve, discarding the seeds and skins, and collecting the fruit pulp in a bowl.

Return the pulp to the saucepan and add the sugar. Bring back to the boil, stirring all the time, and reduce the heat to simmer for 5 minutes. Remove from the heat, and put aside to cool.

Place the cream into a mixing bowl and whisk until stiff. Add the vanilla extract and the condensed milk and whisk again, mixing the ingredients thoroughly and aerating them. The little bubbles trapped in the cream mixture help to make the frozen ice cream soft.

Pour the cream mixture into a freezer-safe tub and divide down the middle with a spatula. Pour half the rosehip mixture into the groove and stir broadly in figure-of-eight motions, then add the other half and stir in around the edges of the tub. Put the lid on the tub and place in the freezer. The ice cream will be ready in a minimum of 3 hours and should be taken out of the freezer 10 minutes before serving.

Try this basic recipe with different fruit purées, such as haw, apple, pear, wineberry or autumn olive. The ice cream is very sweet, so you may not need to add sugar to the fruit – the contrast of sweet, creamy ice cream with a tart fruit ripple is just perfect!

Autumn olive
(*Elaeagnus umbellata*)

A top plant in the forest garden, this deciduous large shrub is an excellent windbreak, bee plant and nitrogen fixer, and also produces a crop of fantastic fruits.

When they first turn red, the fruits will still be slightly astringent, but this disappears on cooking or drying. Autumn olive jam and fruit leathers are always favourites on forest gardening courses.

The fruit contains about 8.3 per cent sugars, 4.5 per cent protein and 12mg per 100g vitamin C. It was recently discovered that they also contain high amounts of lycopene, a carotenoid pigment most commonly associated with tomato and considered an important phytonutrient, thought to prevent or fight cancer of the prostate, mouth, throat and skin, and to reduce the risk of cardiovascular disease. The lycopene content of autumn olive fruit averages about 40-50mg/100g, compared with 3mg/100g for fresh raw tomato and 10mg/100g for canned whole tomato. Because of the high lycopene levels in autumn olive fruit, and the potential health benefits of this phytonutrient, there has been increased interest in commercial fruit production.

Autumn olive leafs out in late winter and retains its leaves late into the autumn, so as a shelter and windbreak plant it is excellent. The reddish speckled fruits ripen in September/October. An individual bush will ripen fruits over 3-4 weeks, and the ripe fruits can hang well on the bushes if birds don't take them. There are also earlier- and later-ripening selections of autumn olive to make the season longer.

Although individual fruits are small (about 10mm/¼" across), they are borne in profusion, lining the branches thickly, and it is a fast crop to harvest by picking or by shaking the bushes. The fruits store for about 2 weeks in a fridge or can be placed straight into a freezer to use at a later date. In size and texture they are similar to currants and blueberries and can be used in the same way in desserts such as pavlovas and cheesecakes, in stewed fruit mixtures or on top of pastries.

Autumn olive & red onion relish

200g (7oz) autumn olives

2 red onions, finely shredded

2 tbsp vegetable oil

3 garlic cloves, crushed

5cm (2") piece fresh ginger, peeled and finely grated

150ml (5¼fl oz) fruit vinegar

140g (5oz) light muscovado sugar

½ tsp ground nutmeg

½ tsp ground cinnamon

½ tsp ground cardamom

In a heavy-based saucepan, fry the onions in the oil over a medium heat for about 5 minutes, until they are translucent and beginning to brown. Add the garlic and ginger and fry for 1 minute, then add all the remaining ingredients apart from the autumn olives. Bring to the boil then reduce the heat and simmer for 5 minutes.

Add the autumn olives and simmer for a further 5 minutes. Stir occasionally but take care to keep the berries intact, and remove from the heat before they break down.

Transfer to a sterilised storage jar and store in the fridge. The relish will keep for up to 3 weeks.

Autumn olive & blackberry tartlets

Makes about 12 tartlets

200g (7oz) autumn olives
100g (3½oz) blackberries
1 tbsp berry jam
1 tbsp hot water

Pastry:
225g (8oz) plain flour, sifted
100g (3½oz) butter, diced and at room temperature
80g (2¾oz) golden caster sugar
1 egg, whisked
A little milk (if needed)

Crème pâtissière:
250ml (8¾fl oz) whole milk
3 drops vanilla essence
3 eggs, yolks only
60g (2oz) caster sugar
30g (1oz) plain flour

Optional – autumn olive purée topping:
50g (1¾oz) caster sugar
1 tbsp cornflour

Baking beans (dried beans or lentils)
A 12-cup cake tin
9cm (3½") pastry cutter

Preheat the oven to 180°C (350°F / Gas Mark 4)

Autumn olives, like other berries, contain small, hard seeds. They are no more noticeable than those in other berries, but if you would rather avoid them you can choose to make a purée topping from the autumn olives rather than using them whole, as described below.

For the pastry, work the butter into the flour to achieve a crumb texture. Add the caster sugar and stir in. Add the egg and combine all ingredients together into a single ball, adding a little milk if necessary. Wrap the ball of dough in cling film and refrigerate for at least 20 minutes.

Dust a surface with flour and roll the pastry dough out to about 4mm (⅛") thick. Using the pastry cutter, cut out 12 discs of pastry and place them into the depressions of the cake tin. Prick each case with a fork, place a layer of foil or baking parchment over the pastry and fill with dried beans or lentils (baking beans), which will provide weight to prevent the pastry from lifting away from the bottom of the dish as it cooks. Bake for 15-20 minutes, remove from oven, and remove the beans and foil/parchment. Allow to cool in the tin.

For the crème pâtissière, combine the milk and vanilla essence in a saucepan and warm over a low heat until it begins to steam. In a mixing bowl combine the egg, sugar and flour to form a coarse paste. Slowly add the warm milk and whisk into a smooth liquid. Return the mixture to the saucepan and place over a low heat, stirring continuously with a whisk, until the mixture thickens.

While the crème is still hot, spoon it into the pastry cases, leaving enough space to put the berries on top. If using the autumn olives whole, arrange them on top of the crème and top with two or three blackberries. If you would prefer to make a purée, blend the autumn olives and sieve out the seeds and pulp to form a thick juice. Place the juice in a small saucepan with the sugar and cornflour. Over a low heat stir continuously until the purée thickens. Remove from the heat and spoon a little purée on top of the crème in each tartlet. Top with two or three blackberries and allow to cool.

Mix together the jam and hot water and glaze the tartlets with a pastry brush. Leave to cool and serve when ready.

Chestnuts (*Castanea* spp.)

Sweet chestnut is well known as a commercial crop in some countries, particularly in the Mediterranean, but increasing numbers of people are growing suitable selections in the UK and other cooler regions. It tends to be a more reliable crop than many nuts, because the trees flower in summer, so frosts are never a problem.

Fresh chestnuts are perishable and do not store well for very long – just a few weeks at cool temperatures in an airy place. To use them fresh in cooking, they need shelling/peeling. The easiest way to do this is to cut the nuts in half, then boil them for about 5 minutes, after which the half kernels should separate quite easily from the shell and thin inner shell.

If you dry chestnuts in-shell, they will store for years. The outer shells are brittle, so to shell them, put some in a bag or sack and whack it against the floor a few times; you can then pick out the kernel pieces from the mixture. The dry kernels should be soaked overnight and boiled for 40-50 minutes to cook (less if they are added to other recipes which are cooked further).

Chestnuts, as well as being a high-carbohydrate food, are a good source of vitamin C, and are high in minerals including potassium and manganese.

The nuts can ripen between late September and early November in the UK, depending on the selection. Obviously, further north, early-season varieties are more suitable, as these do not require a long growing season.

As with most nuts, chestnuts are harvested from the ground after they have dropped from the tree. However, they contain much more water (about 60 per cent in total) than other nuts, which makes them more perishable – this means it is more important to harvest daily, as chestnuts on the ground will start to rot more quickly. It is also important to use the nuts quickly, as – apart from drying (see page 40) – long-term storage is not easy. It is also worth sorting through your chestnuts to make sure there are none with holes in them, which indicates a pesky maggot inside.

Chestnut & lentil pâté

This pâté is a favourite on forest gardening courses and is really easy to make.

100g (3½oz) fresh chestnuts or 50g (1¾oz) dried chestnuts

340g (12oz) onions, diced

2 tbsp olive oil

2 garlic cloves, crushed

150g (5¼oz) red split lentils

500ml (18fl oz) vegetable stock

Salt and pepper

Stick blender

With fresh chestnuts, halve and cook for 5-10 minutes, then peel off the outer and inner shells. If starting with dried chestnuts, soak these overnight and boil for 40 minutes.

Fry the onions in the oil over a medium heat until browned. Add the crushed garlic cloves and lentils, stirring for a minute or two so the lentils get coated with oil.

Add the vegetable stock (you could use Kallo vegan wheat-free stock cubes) and bring to the boil. Place the lid on the pan and simmer for 20 minutes until the lentils are soft and fully cooked.

Now add the chestnut pieces, stir well and remove from the heat. Use a stick blender to purée the mixture; check seasoning, then place it in a bowl.

Pheasant pot roast with quince & chestnuts

Serves 2-3

150g (5¼oz) quince, puréed (see method)

200g (7oz) chestnuts

2 tbsp olive oil

30g (1oz) butter

1 medium red onion, finely sliced

80g (2¾oz) mushrooms, finely sliced

50g (1¾oz) chorizo or smoked bacon, finely sliced

1 pheasant, skinned and prepared

1 tbsp plain flour

300ml (10½fl oz) chicken stock

2 tbsp chopped fresh rosemary

2 tbsp chopped fresh sage

Salt and pepper

Stick blender

Heat the oil and butter in a large frying pan. Add the onion, mushrooms and chorizo. Rinse the pheasant through with cold running water and place on its side in the middle of the pan, surrounded by the other ingredients. Over a medium heat, lightly brown the pheasant on both sides, then remove from the pan and place into a preheated slow cooker on high. If you don't have a slow cooker you can use a casserole dish – pre-heat the oven to 150°C (300°F / Gas Mark 2)

With the heat off, add the flour to the pan and stir into the ingredients, coating them evenly. Now add the stock, slowly stirring it into combine with the flour. Finally stir in the quince purée and transfer the mix to the slow cooker, surrounding the pheasant. Add the chestnuts and herbs and replace the lid.

Cook for 3-4 hours in the slow cooker, or 1-2 hours in the oven, until the meat is fully cooked and tender. Periodically turn the pheasant and baste with some of the sauce to keep the meat moist. Check seasoning.

Serve with potatoes and steamed greens for a warming autumnal feast!

For the puréed quince:
Peel, core and dice the quinces (roughly twice the weight of whole fruit of the final weight of purée required); place into a saucepan and cover with water. Bring to the boil and then simmer gently until the quinces are soft and drop off smoothly when you push a fork into them. Strain off excess water (you can leave in a little water for a finer purée) and blend with a stick blender until smooth.

Try this with other birds, such as wood pigeon or duck. The tartness of the quinces and the sweetness of the chestnuts complement their rich, earthy flavours.

Sweet chestnut pastry

Makes about 12 pastries or a 25cm (10") flan

100g (3½oz) sweet chestnut flour (see right)
110g (3¾oz) butter
50g (1¾oz) caster sugar
1 egg, beaten
100g (3½oz) plain white flour
A little milk (if needed)

Garnish:
Fresh chestnuts, halved

Preheat the oven to 180°C (350°F / Gas Mark 4)

Whisk together the butter and sugar until creamy. Gently whisk in the egg, then add the chestnut flour and sieve in the plain flour. Fold together with a spoon until it begins to bind, adding a splash of milk if necessary to keep it moist, then flour your hands and roll the mixture into a firm ball. Flatten to a disc and wrap in cling film, then put in the fridge for 10 minutes.

When the pastry has cooled and settled it will be ready to roll out on a floured surface and used for sweet pies, flans and tarts.

For the flour:
Whole dried sweet chestnuts (see page 40 for drying advice) are too large to put through a normal grain mill, so break them up into pieces. The best way to do this is put them into a cloth bag or sack and break them against a concrete floor with a hammer! The pieces, which can be a little larger than grains, will then go through most grain mills to produce chestnut flour. See Resources for suppliers of grain mills.

Try this with puréed medlars to make chestnut and medlar tartlets:

Roll out half the above quantity of pastry to 4mm (¹/₈″) thick. Using a small round pastry cutter, cut out circles of pastry and push them into a 12-cup cake tin.

Spoon in medlar purée to half-fill the pastry cases. Peel and halve fresh chestnuts to garnish, and brush the pastry crusts and chestnuts with honey water (1 tsp honey + ¹/₂ tsp hot water).

Bake for 25 minutes or until the crusts have browned.

 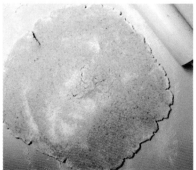 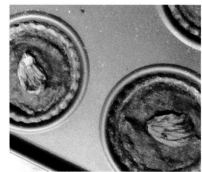

Flowering quince / japonica (*Chaenomeles japonica*)

Flowering quinces are mainly treated as ornamentals in the UK, but are valuable fruiting plants, and japonica (*C. japonica*) is known as the northern lemon in the Baltic states, where it is grown commercially.

Japonica is the smallest of the *Chaenomeles*, growing around 1m (3') high and wide. Pink or reddish flowers in spring are followed by greenish-yellow fruits that ripen in autumn and hang well on the bushes.

The fruits and juice are acid and, for most people, need sweetening; they are very high in vitamin C and high in potassium.

Harvest the fruits in autumn. They are 3-6cm (1¼-2½") in diameter and contain a number of dark brown seeds. In common with apples and other members of the Rosaceae, these seeds are poisonous and should not be eaten.

Quinceade

Makes 4.5l (8 pints / 160fl oz)

710g (1lb 9oz) japonica fruits

4l (7 pints / 140fl oz) water

300g (10½oz) sugar or equivalent sweetener (less or more to taste)

This is a superb soft drink. You can use fresh fruits but you can also use the previous year's harvest that has been put straight in the freezer with no treatment.

Halve fruits and remove seeds, using the handle end of a teaspoon to scoop them out. Place the halves in a liquidiser with about 710ml (1¼ pints / 25fl oz) of water and liquidise for a few seconds. Pour into a sieve over a bowl and slowly pour on 2.5l (4½ pints / 90fl oz) more water, agitating the pulp so that you are extracting the maximum flavour from it.

Boil the remaining water and dissolve the sugar, then add to the juice. Bottle and use within a few days.

Other recipes using flowering quince: Baked American elderflower custard with flowering quince compote (page 110); Flowering quince & haw chutney (Part 1, page 23).

Hawthorns (*Crataegus* spp.)

There are numerous hawthorn species, many of which have excellent fruits for eating. Most form small trees with abundant ornamental flowers in spring. They are easy trees to grow in most situations.

The young leaves are also eaten in spring, mainly in salads. The fruits, usually red or orange, ripen in September/October. They hold well on the tree so it is worth waiting until most or all are ripe, then harvesting in one go. They can be made into haw jam and included in fruit leather mixes.

Haw fruits contain useful quantities of vitamins B and C, as well as many minerals.

To de-seed fruits like haws, with relatively small seeds, you can use a Moulinex sieve: fix a plate with appropriate-sized holes in the base, then put in the fruits or fruit pulp and turn the handle to force the pulp through the holes. Softer haws can be put straight into the sieve, though firmer ones may need simmering for a few minutes to soften them.

Roasted wild duck with haw and chestnut stuffing

Serves 2

1 tbsp haw jelly (see Part 1, page 20)
1 prepared wild duck (590-710g / 1lb 5oz-1lb 9oz)

Stuffing:
1 tsp haw jelly
50g (1¾oz) fresh chestnuts
40g (1½oz) stale bread
1 tsp dried sage
Half a small onion / 1 long welsh onion leaf, chopped
Vegetable oil
1 small egg, beaten
Salt and pepper

Garnish:
3 large sage leaves

Food processor

Preheat the oven to 150°C (300°F, Gas Mark 2)

Take the prepared duck and rinse thoroughly, outside and inside, with cold water. Pat it dry with kitchen paper and place in the centre of a roasting tin.

To make the stuffing, put the bread, chestnuts and sage into a food processor and blend to a chunky crumb consistency. Fry the onion gently in a little oil until translucent (you don't need to fry welsh onion). Transfer the onion and crumb mix to a mixing bowl and add the teaspoon of haw jelly, egg, salt and pepper to taste. Stir together well until you can form a ball with the mixture, ensuring the egg and jelly have been well combined. If your bread was very dry you may wish to add the hot water to get the mixture to stick together, but if your ball is firm you won't need it – the cooking juices of the duck will moisten the stuffing as it cooks.

Using a tablespoon, spoon the stuffing into the cavity of the duck. Prick the skin in a few places with a sharp knife to allow the fat to self-baste the duck while cooking. Put 1 tablespoon of haw jelly into a cup, add half a tablespoon of hot water and stir until the jelly has dissolved. Using a pastry brush, glaze the duck liberally with the haw jelly, then lay the sage leaves across the top as a garnish.

Put in the centre of the oven and roast for 50 minutes, or until the juices run clear and the skin is well browned. Remove after 20 minutes to re-glaze and add some parboiled potatoes to roast around the bird. Allow it to rest on a carving board for 10 minutes after cooking. While the duck rests you can drain any excess oil from the roasting tin to make gravy, then return your potatoes to the oven at 200°C (400°F / Gas Mark 6) to crisp up.

Try this with pheasant and replace the haw jelly with quince jam, and the sage with rosemary.

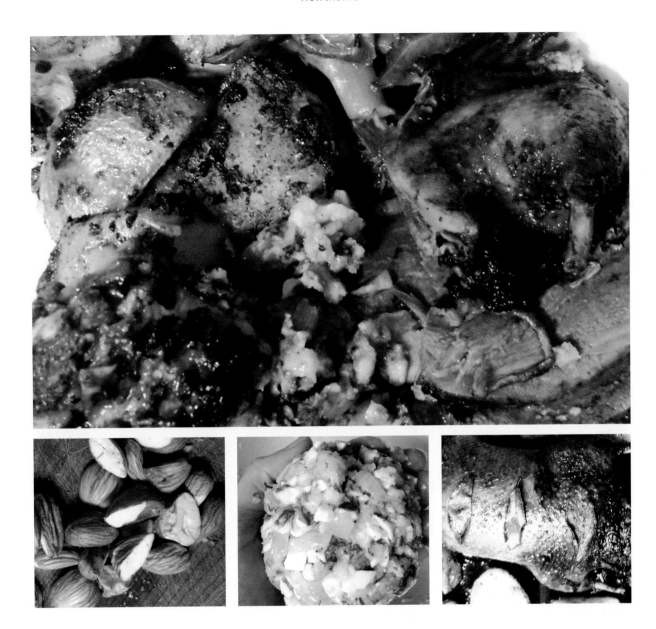

To make traditional gravy

If you are not roasting vegetables in the same tin, or if the vegetables are ready when the bird comes out of the oven, you can make gravy in the roasting tin. Otherwise, just drain off the oil and juices into a saucepan. Add 1 tbsp plain flour and stir into the oil with a wooden spoon or a hand whisk until fully blended. Turn on to a low heat and allow the flour and oil to cook gently for 2 minutes, stirring continuously. Now add the vegetable water (the trick is to remember to keep it when straining the veg!) a little at a time, making sure you have blended it well before adding more. You can add a stock cube to the water first for more flavour, and a drop of gravy browning or yeast extract for colour. Bring the gravy to the boil and simmer gently for 5 minutes. Serve in a preheated jug.

Haw & apple strudel

Serves 4-6

400g (14oz) haws
400g (14oz) eating apples, cored and diced
50g (1¾oz) sultanas
¼ tsp ground nutmeg
6 sheets filo pastry
50g (1¾oz) melted butter
2 tsp Demerara sugar

Preheat the oven to 190°C (375°F, Gas Mark 5)

Prepare your haws by gently cooking them whole over a low heat for around 15 minutes. If they are fairly hard, add 1cm (½") of water to the pan and cover to simmer gently. Remove from the heat and allow to cool. Once cooled, mash them with a potato masher or a pestle to release the pulp. Transfer to a large sieve and, using a pestle or a wooden spoon, push the pulp through the sieve into a bowl, a spoonful at a time, discarding the skin and seeds as you go (or use a Moulinex sieve as described on page 163). Put the pulped haws to one side.

Place the apples into a spacious saucepan. Eating apples do not need sugar or water adding. Place over a low heat and cover, stirring occasionally, for 5-10 minutes or until the apples have become soft. You can keep the apples fairly chunky for this recipe – just remove them from the heat before they break down completely. Add the haw pulp, sultanas and nutmeg to the apples and stir together well. The haw pulp binds the mixture and gives a pleasant rosy tint.

Put a sheet of baking parchment or kitchen foil on your work surface and lay out the first sheet of pastry. Brush the sheet with melted butter and carefully place the second sheet on top. Brush the second sheet and repeat until all sheets are on top of one another, stuck together with butter. Now place your fruit mixture in a thick line in the centre of the pastry. Fold the top edge over the fruit and brush with butter, then fold the bottom edge over and brush with butter, then fold in the side edges to close up the parcel. Using the paper or foil, gently roll the parcel upside down on to a greased baking tray to reveal what will be the top of your strudel. With a knife, cut slits widthways along the length of the parcel, brush with butter and sprinkle with the sugar.

Place the tray in the top of the oven and bake for 30 minutes, or until the top is golden and crispy. Serve warm with cream, ice cream or yogurt.

Try this with apple and medlar, apple and quince or apple and pear. Filo pastry is easy to find in most supermarkets, but if you have the time and the inclination, it is a good challenge to make it yourself. If you make a batch you can freeze it between layers of baking parchment in readiness for the tree fruit harvests.

Other recipes using hawthorn: Spring forest salad (page 70); Haw jelly (Part 1, page 20); Flowering quince and haw chutney (Part 1, page 23).

Hazels (*Corylus* spp.)

The only native nut to the UK, this is ironically probably the least used in cooking! Hazel trees are well known from hedgerows and woodlands, where they make large shrubs or small trees, and the crop of nuts is – if you can get it before critters like squirrels – extremely versatile. Hazelnuts are high in healthy fats (oils), protein, iron, calcium, vitamins C, E, etc. Commonly used in sweet recipes, they are particularly good with milk chocolate and used in desserts, but they are also very good in savoury dishes. When added to a casserole they become soft, like chestnuts.

The nuts ripen in September and are best shaken from the trees and collected from the ground using a Nut Wizard (see page 15), or shaken on to a tarp or sheet. They will need drying to store (in-shell is best), after which they will store for several years at room temperature.

Hazel trees are often biennial in their cropping nature, with a heavy crop year alternating with a light or no crop year. This goes for wild trees as well as the cultivated types you might deliberately have planted. Squirrel problems are always worse when wild trees are having a light year, whereas if a heavy crop year in wild trees coincides with a heavy crop year on your cultivated trees, the squirrels may leave yours alone. May. Or may not.

Ricotta, honeycomb, hazelnuts

This recipe by Hugh Fearnley-Whittingstall is a delicious way to eat hazelnuts. You probably won't get honeycomb at your local supermarket, but good delis often stock it, and a small local honey producer will be able to sell to you direct; it's also available online. It's worth getting hold of some because it is such a treat: honey in its purest form, straight from the hive, untreated and pretty much as the bees intended it. The idea is to eat the whole thing, comb and all. The comb has a chewy, waxy texture and is perfectly edible, but you can discreetly discard the chewed comb once you've sucked all the honey from it, if you prefer.

Serves 4

100g (3½oz) hazelnuts (skin-on)
255g (9oz) ricotta
About 200g (7oz) honeycomb

Preheat the oven to 180°C (350°F / Gas Mark 4)

Spread the hazelnuts out on a baking sheet and toast them in the oven for about 5 minutes, until they are lightly coloured and their skins are starting to split. Tip them on to a clean tea towel, fold the towel over them and give them a vigorous rub. This will remove most of the skins – don't worry if a few bits remain. Alternatively, you can remove the skins by tipping the hazelnuts into a sieve and rubbing the tea towel over them, so the bits of skin fall through the sieve.

Divide the ricotta between shallow serving bowls. Break or cut your honeycomb into four roughly equal pieces and place on the ricotta, trickling over any honey that has escaped from the comb too. Scatter over the hazelnuts. Admire the irresistible tripartite simplicity of what you have just compiled, and serve with a smile.

You can use a thick, rich natural yogurt instead of the ricotta, or plain fromage frais. And, of course, you can use a good runny honey without the comb.

Hazelnut & mulberry shortbread

Makes 20 biscuits

80g (2¾oz) hazelnuts
40g (1½oz) dried mulberries
130g (4½oz) butter, at room temperature
60g (2oz) golden caster sugar
120g (4¼oz) plain white flour
50g (1¾oz) sweet chestnut flour or rice flour
½ tsp allspice
Pinch of salt
Icing sugar

A 6cm (2½") pastry cutter

Food processor

Preheat the oven to 150°C (300°F, Gas Mark 2)

Toast the hazelnuts in the oven for 5 minutes on a baking tray. Remove from the oven and allow to cool. Once cooled you should be able to remove the skins easily by rubbing them between your fingers or as described opposite. Transfer the skinned nuts to a food processor and roughly chop so that you have varying sizes of hazelnut chunks.

Using a spoon or an electric whisk, cream the butter and sugar until soft and light. Sift in the plain flour, chestnut flour, allspice and salt. Using your fingertips work the ingredients together until they form a soft crumb texture. Add the hazelnuts and mulberries, and if the mixture seems too dry add a little more butter and mix into the dough. Keep the mixture loose and crumb-like until you feel you have the right consistency to form a cohesive, malleable ball. Take care not to overwork the mixture, and be as gentle and sparing as possible with your mixing to keep the dough light. When you are happy with the consistency, gently press the dough together into one ball.

Transfer to a flour-dusted surface and press the ball into a flat disc. Using a flour-dusted rolling pin, roll the dough out to about 1cm (⅜") thick. Cut out biscuits with the pastry cutter, then gather up the excess dough into a ball, roll it out and cut again. Line a flat baking tray with baking parchment and carefully transfer the biscuits to the tray using a palette knife.

Bake for 20 minutes in the centre of the oven. If your oven is hotter at the back, you may want to turn the tray halfway through to prevent those at the back from burning. Remove from the oven and allow to cool on the tray for a few minutes before transferring to a cooling rack. When cool, dust with icing sugar.

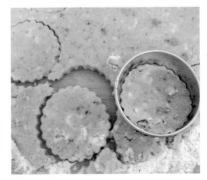

Squirrel with wild mushrooms & hazelnuts

As one of the biggest hindrances to a good hazelnut crop is the grey squirrel, it seems fitting to put them together in this hearty autumnal stew!

Serves 2

2 squirrels, prepared and jointed

80g (2¾oz) hazelnuts, toasted and skinned

50g (1¾oz) plain flour, seasoned

30g (1oz) butter

2 tbsp olive oil

1 medium onion, diced

300g (10½oz) mixed mushrooms (e.g. chanterelle, hedgehog, oyster, field, wood cep), sliced

2 garlic cloves, crushed

200ml (7fl oz) white wine

600ml (21fl oz) chicken or vegetable stock

2 sprigs of thyme, leaves stripped

1 tbsp fresh chopped sage

80ml (3fl oz) double cream

Salt and pepper

Place the seasoned flour in a shallow dish and roll the squirrel pieces in it until well covered.

Add the butter and oil to a spacious, heavy-based saucepan and place over a medium heat until the butter has melted. Add the onion and mushrooms and fry for about 2 minutes, until they begin to soften, then add the garlic and fry for 1 minute more. Add the squirrel pieces and brown lightly on all sides. Add a tablespoon of the remaining seasoned flour and stir in until it disappears. Gradually add the wine, stirring continuously, and simmer on a high heat for about 2 minutes. Add the stock, bring to the boil and reduce to a simmer. Add the herbs and hazelnuts and cover the pan.

Leave the pan to simmer on a low heat for 1 hour, and occasionally check that there is enough liquid to cover the meat and vegetables; add more stock if necessary. After 1 hour the meat should start to come off the bone. If it is still clinging to the bone continue cooking for up to 30 minutes, checking occasionally until the meat is really tender. When ready, remove the pan from the heat, stir in the cream and season to taste.

Serve with boiled or mashed potatoes and some seasonal greens.

Hazelnuts are more palatable cooked than raw – roasting lightly is one of the best ways. Like this they are also a fantastic snack food!

Other recipes using hazelnuts: Chicory, pear & hazelnut salad with blue cheese dressing (page 117); Siberian purslane salad (page 217).

Japanese wineberry
(*Rubus phoenicolasius*)

This less common member of the raspberry family grows as a spiny bush about 1.5m (5') high. Like raspberries, its stems are biennial – growing one year, fruiting the next and then dying back – but instead of suckering from the base, Japanese wineberry spreads by tip-layering, like blackberries.

The fruits are likely to be high in vitamins C, E and K, and many minerals, like most of the raspberry-type fruits.

After flowering in spring, the fruits ripen between late July and early September. Before ripening, the fruits are enclosed in papery calyxes, which protect them well against pests. The calyxes open to reveal bright orange-red raspberry-like fruits, which are slightly sticky to the touch. Pick the fruits as they are revealed.

Wineberry & apple mint sorbet

Serves 4-6

450g (1lb) wineberries
A small handful of fresh apple mint
170ml (6fl oz) boiling water
50g (1¾oz) sugar
1 egg white

Garnish:
Apple mint leaves

Tear the apple mint leaves, reserving a few for garnish, and put them into a measuring jug. Pour over the boiling water and allow to steep until cool.

Either mash or blend the wineberries in a liquidiser until puréed. Pour the purée through a sieve into a bowl and discard the seeds and pulp. Strain the mint leaves from the water and add the water and sugar to the wineberry juice. Stir together well and transfer to a plastic, freezer-safe storage container. Check the sorbet periodically and remove when it is semi-frozen – solid at the edges and slushy in the middle.

Whisk the egg white until it forms stiff peaks. When the sorbet is semi-frozen, remove it from the freezer and add it to the egg white. Whisk together briefly and return to the container, and then to the freezer.

The sorbet is ready to eat once it is completely frozen, but you may want to remove it from the freezer 10-20 minutes before eating so it is easier to scoop. Decorate with apple mint leaves and serve.

This basic sorbet recipe works well with any fruit or combination of fruits. You may need to alter the amount of sugar you use, depending on the tartness of the fruit you choose, and some fruits will benefit from being cooked so that you can make a smooth purée. Delicious combinations include black-currant and apple, wineberry and melon, and autumn olive and mulberry.

Wineberry meringues with hazelnuts

Serves 6-8

300g (10½oz) wineberries
2 egg whites
130g (4½oz) golden caster sugar
285ml (½ pint / 10fl oz) double cream, whipped

Garnish
30g (1oz) hazelnuts, toasted and chopped

Muslin

Preheat the oven to 140°C (275°F / Gas Mark 1)

Line a baking tray with baking parchment. In a spacious mixing bowl, whisk the egg whites until they form stiff peaks. Whisk in the caster sugar one tablespoon at a time, leaving one tablespoon aside for the fruit coulis. Whisk until thick and glossy, then place individual spoonfuls on to the baking parchment, making 16 little meringues.

Place the tray in the centre of the oven and bake for 1 hour. To test if the meringues are fully cooked, lift one and tap the base. It should be hard and sound hollow. Remove the meringues from the oven and place on a rack to cool.

Meanwhile, whip the cream and refrigerate until needed. Add the reserved tablespoon of sugar to half of the wineberries and either mash or use a liquidiser to blend them to a purée. Sieve into a bowl or strain through muslin to remove the seeds, then refrigerate until needed.

Assemble the dessert just before serving. Place a good spoonful of whipped cream into the bottom of each dessert bowl, then top with two or three meringues. Sprinkle over some whole wineberries, drizzle with coulis and top with hazelnuts.

Try this with other forest garden berries or a mix of several, including autumn olives, mulberries, blackcurrants or raspberries. You could use other nuts, too, and try blending these to a coarse powder and folding them into the meringue mix before cooking, for a different texture.

Medlar *(Mespilus germanica)*

Medlars make small, often twisted fruit trees. They flower in late May, after frosts have finished, so tend to be very reliable croppers. The fruits have a distinctive shape, like a sphere with an edge cut off flat, and can grow to 3-4cm (approx. 1-1½") diameter on good-fruiting varieties.

The texture of ripe fruits is like a purée, and the flavour is sweet with elements of date and apple. Some people enjoy them raw; they can also be used to make medlar jam and included in fruit leathers (they are good mixed with a juicier fruit). They are high in vitamin A, phosphorus and potassium.

Traditionally, the fruits are harvested still unripe with the first frosts in autumn; however, in warm summers in Devon they start ripening on the tree – a climate change effect. Conventional wisdom dictates that the fruits should be 'bletted' – a process that involves ripening them until they are semi-rotten – but not all would agree. When they ripen, the fruits soften and darken in colour. In cool Devon summers the fruit can still be harvested in late October, when the first frosts arrive; if they are placed indoors in a cool place, they will ripen 1-2 weeks later.

Medlar & walnut slices

200g (7oz) medlars

200ml (7fl oz) water

3 tsp brown sugar

130g (4½oz) butter, at room temperature

130g (4½oz) caster sugar

100g (3½oz) ground walnuts

¼ tsp cinnamon

200g (7oz) plain flour

1 egg, beaten

50g (1¾oz) chopped walnuts

1 tbsp brown sugar

Milk

Baking tin approx. 25 x 30cm (10 x 12") and at least 4cm (1½") deep.

Preheat the oven to 190°C (375°F / Gas Mark 5)

Place the medlars in a saucepan with the water and 3 teaspoons of brown sugar. Bring to the boil and simmer until they break up. Remove from the heat and strain off the water, then place a sieve over a bowl and push the pulp through with a wooden spoon, leaving the skin and seeds in the sieve to be discarded. Put the pulp to one side while you make your dough.

Slice the butter into a mixing bowl, add the caster sugar, ground walnuts and cinnamon and sieve in the flour. Rub the ingredients together to form a crumb, then make a space in the middle of the mixture and add the egg. Using a wooden spoon gradually mix the crumb into the egg to form a dough. Stir in milk a splash at a time until the dough reaches a thick 'dropping' consistency. Place half the dough into the centre of the greased baking tin. Level out the dough across the tin using a spatula. Now spoon the medlar pulp on top and spread over in an even layer.

Sprinkle half of the chopped walnuts over the medlar layer and cover with the second half of the dough mix. This forms a sandwich of two layers of dough with medlar and walnuts in the centre. Finish by sprinkling the top with the remaining chopped walnuts and the brown sugar.

Bake for 15-20 minutes. Remove and allow to cool, then slice into squares and store in a sandwich box for snacks and teatime treats.

Try this with haws instead of medlars. This version is based on a traditional recipe using mincemeat as the middle layer, but works well with tart, pulpy fruits such as medlars and haws, with a little spice such as cinnamon or nutmeg and some chopped nuts.

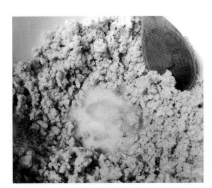

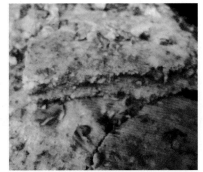

Toffee medlars

200g (7oz) medlars, bletted
60g (2oz) butter
80g (2¾oz) caster sugar
¼ tsp ground cinnamon
¼ tsp ground nutmeg

Preheat the oven to 200°C (400°F / Gas Mark 6)

Melt the butter in a large frying pan, add the medlars and fry on a medium heat for 5 minutes. Turn off the heat and add the sugar and spices. Stir together well, covering the medlars as much as possible. Transfer into a baking dish and put into the oven for 10-15 minutes, until the medlars are browned and the skin has begun to split. The sugar forms a toffee coating on the medlars, which will be very hot when they come out of the oven, so allow to cool a little and serve warm with ice cream.

Try this with chestnuts and walnuts. Peel or crack the nuts and add them raw to the sugar and butter mix, then bake as above. For a sweet snack with a lower glycaemic index, use honey instead of sugar as follows:

60g (2oz) butter
2 tbsp honey
¼ tsp ground cinnamon
¼ tsp ground nutmeg

Melt the butter in a saucepan, add the honey and spices and stir together until combined. Add your medlars and/or nuts and stir together, coating with the honey mixture. Transfer to a baking dish and bake at 180°C (350°F / Gas Mark 4) for 15 minutes.

Oaks (*Quercus* spp.)

Acorns of all oak species can be used for food, but most of them contain high levels of tannins, which are poisonous so must be removed before eating.

A number of cultures have depended on acorns as a staple in the past, and luckily there are still several well-documented ways of removing tannins. Cold-water leaching (described overleaf) is a good method and leads to minimal nutrient loss. You can also boil chopped acorn meal in water for faster removal, but you will lose more nutrients that way.

Acorns provide a complete vegetable protein and are high in carbohydrates. They contain 16 amino acids, appreciable amounts of vitamins A and C, and significant quantities of calcium, magnesium, phosphorus, potassium and sulphur.

As with most nuts, acorns are harvested from the ground. The first acorns to drop from a tree will usually have holes drilled in them and are being consumed within by nut weevils, so do not harvest these! Ideally clear them away before the good acorns start to fall. If you have poultry they will love to consume any weevil larvae emerging from the infested nuts.

Acorn preparation

After harvesting acorns, leave them in a cool, dry place for 1-2 weeks. This will encourage the kernels to shrink slightly, making shelling easier, and allow the tannin levels to reduce.

Shelling acorns can be done in a number of ways. For a fairly small number – as required in the recipes here – just cut each acorn in half lengthways with a sharp knife, and the two halves of the kernel will fall out freely. For larger quantities you can crush the acorns on a wooden board with a wooden mallet or piece of wood – this is messier and you have to separate out the bits of shell afterwards. If the acorns have been dried, you can put them through a nut-cracking machine (either hand-cranked or powered).

Removing the tannins from acorns is easy, and is no more trouble than (say) the sprouting of seeds.

Grind the acorn kernels into small pieces (2-6mm – less than ¼") in a coffee grinder or food blender. Half-fill a large jar with the acorn meal and fill to the top with fresh water. Place in a fridge. Then empty off the water from the top half of the jar and refill with fresh water twice a day for 3-4 days. Initially the water will be brown, as the tannins leach out of the acorns, but it becomes clearer day by day. After 3 or 4 days, the tannins have all gone, and the acorn meal can be drained off and then used.

You can leach tannins more quickly by repeatedly boiling the acorn meal and draining, but you are likely to lose many more nutrients this way, and the acorn meal also ends up a much darker-brown colour.

To make acorn flour, spread the acorn meal on a non-stick baking sheet to allow it to dry, and mill it into flour. Hawos (see Resources section) make fantastic small stone mills.

Starch extraction

Extracting the starch involves an adaption of the leaching method described above. As you pour off the tannin water from your soaked acorn grits, pay attention to a creamy, cloudy substance in the water – this is the starch. Stop pouring once this starts to flow, top up with fresh water and soak again for a few hours. To keep the starch, you have to leach the acorns for longer (as you are not pouring off as much at each change of water), ensuring that you do not pour any of the cloudy starch out in the process. After a few days, when the acorns are ripe, fill the container with water once more, stir well and allow to settle for 1 hour. Pour the clear water off and pour the cloudy water into a separate bowl, add fresh water to the acorns and allow to settle again, adding any cloudy water from this second round to the first.

Allow the starchy water to stand for 1 hour then separate, pouring off the clear water, and you should be left with an off-white, slightly sticky substance which can be dried in a very low oven or dehydrator to make acorn starch flour.

Acorn shortbread cookies

Makes 20 cookies

50g (1¾oz) acorn flour
150g (5¼oz) plain flour
60g (2oz) caster sugar
150g (5¼oz) margarine or butter

Preheat the oven to 180°C (350°F / Gas Mark 4).

Mix all the ingredients in a bowl, working the margarine or butter in with your fingertips.

Fashion small balls with your hands, place on to a greased baking tray and flatten gently (the mixture is too sticky to be able to spoon out effectively.)

Bake for 10-15 minutes until the cookies just start to brown. Remove and place on a cooling rack.

Acorn soup

This is a thick, rich and nutty soup which is filling and warming – perfect for a chilly autumn day.

Serves 4-6

200g (7oz) fresh acorns, leached
1 onion, finely chopped
1 small leek, finely chopped
2 tbsp olive oil
100g (3½oz) swede, diced
100g (3½oz) potatoes, diced
1.25l (2¼ pints / 44fl oz) vegetable stock
Small sprig of fresh rosemary, leaves stripped from the twig
2 fresh sage leaves

To serve:
Crème fraîche to serve

Stick blender

Place the onion and leek in a large saucepan with the olive oil and fry gently until soft. Add the swede, potatoes and acorns to the saucepan and fry for a further 3 minutes.

Add the vegetable stock and simmer on a low heat for 15 minutes. Add the rosemary and sage leaves

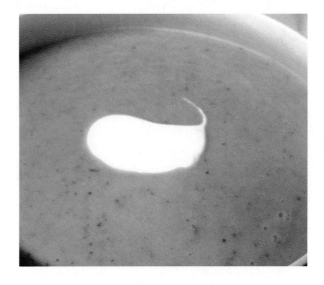

and simmer for a further 5 minutes.

Remove from the heat and blend to a smooth consistency using a stick blender. Season to taste.

Serve with a little crème fraîche and a chunk of bread and butter. Goats' cheese complements this soup very well.

Try this with chestnuts seasoned with tarragon and thyme for a rich, sweet alternative.

Acorn pâté

80g (2¾oz) acorns, leached

100g (3½oz) red split lentils

400ml (14fl oz) water

Half a small onion, finely chopped

80g (2¾oz) butter

2 garlic cloves, peeled

½ tsp dried thyme

½ tsp dried tarragon

30g (1oz) breadcrumbs, made from fresh or stale bread

Garnish:

Sprig of thyme

Food processor

Ramekins or small loaf tin

Put the lentils and water in a small saucepan and bring to the boil. Turn down to a simmer, cover and cook for 15 minutes or until completely soft (add more water if needed). Gently fry the onion in 10g (¼oz) butter until soft, then add the remaining butter and remove from the heat as soon as it has melted.

Put the acorns into the food processor and blend to a rough crumb consistency. Add the cooked lentils, butter and onions, garlic, herbs and breadcrumbs to the processor. Blend the ingredients together well until they form a smooth paste. You may need to add a little water to achieve the right consistency, which should be similar to fresh butter icing.

Spread the mixture into the ramekins or loaf tin while it is still warm, smooth over the top with a spatula and garnish with a sprig of thyme. Cover with cling film and place in the fridge to cool and set. Serve with bread or crackers.

Try this with other nuts instead of acorns. It works very well with chestnuts and walnuts, and you could liven it up with some dried redcurrants or berries, and your own combinations of herbs.

Acorn starch panna cotta

This and the following recipe, both from Toni Spencer's Acornucopia project (see www.theferal kitchen.com), work well together. The first uses the starch of the acorn only. The second (overleaf) uses the acorn meal or the 'leftovers' from extracting the starch, without having to dry it.

This panna cotta recipe is inspired by the traditional Korean 'Dotorimuk' (dotori meaning 'acorn'; muk meaning 'jelly'), usually cooked unseasoned and served in a spicy savoury sauce. In Korean supermarkets it is sold ready-made as a block of jelly.

Serves 4-6

100ml (3½fl oz) acorn starch flour (see page 180)

600ml (21fl oz) water (a basic 1:6 ratio of flour to water)

2 tsp good-quality vanilla essence (or contents of one pod)

½ tsp cinnamon

Pinch of salt

1 tbsp cooking oil (sunflower or coconut)

1½ tbsp sugar

Handful of raspberries or blackberries, frozen or fresh

Optional:

1 tsp lemon zest

Ramekins or dessert glasses

Mix the flour and water in a bowl and leave for 10 minutes.

Whisk well and pour into a pan. Bring to a simmer and stir on a low heat for 20-30 minutes. It will thicken suddenly, so keep stirring! Pay attention to the bottom and sides of the pan when stirring, and use a metal spoon (you may need to whisk a little to begin with).

Near the end, add the flavourings, oil and sugar and cook for another few minutes. Stir well.

Fruit can be crushed or crumbled and mixed in at this point, or placed on top of the desserts while they set. Ladle carefully into ramekins or dessert glasses, and leave to set in the fridge for 6 hours or overnight.

This dish is delicious served with whipped cream, melted chocolate or wild fruit coulis.

Acorn burgers

This recipe, also from The Feral Kitchen (see previous page), is very flexible. You can substitute carrots or parsnips for the beetroot (beetroot gives a good pink/meat-like colour) and use any kind of bean. For example, you could use chickpeas and spices to create falafel. This recipe can take more or less acorn depending on availability and taste, and will work without egg.

Serves 6

300g (10½oz) fresh acorn meal or grits

2 medium red onions, finely chopped

1 celery stick

4 garlic cloves

Olive oil

Sprig of fresh sage and rosemary, finely chopped (or 2 tsp each dried)

2 tsp smoked paprika

1 medium or large beetroot

Sea salt & ground black pepper (or Szechuan pepper)

1 240g (8½ oz) tin cooked haricot or black turtle beans

2 tbsp tomato paste

1 large egg

200g (7oz) spelt flour (for coating)

Preheat the oven to 190°C (375°F / Gas Mark 5) if baking the burgers.

Slowly fry the onion, celery and garlic in olive oil until soft, adding the herbs and paprika midway. Grate the beetroot, strain off all the juice and put both aside.

Put aside 100g (3½oz) acorn meal. Put the rest into a pan with a pinch of salt, pepper, 1 tbsp oil and the

beetroot juice and cook for approximately 20 minutes, stirring regularly and topping up with water if necessary to keep it moist.

In another bowl, blend the beans and tomato paste roughly with a potato masher. Once the acorn and beetroot mix has cooled down, mix everything (except the flour) in a large bowl with a good pinch of salt and pepper. Form into patties and coat each one lightly with flour.

Fry in olive oil on a medium heat for approximately 12 minutes each side, or bake in the oven for 25 minutes at 190°C (375°F / Gas Mark 5).

The burgers are delicious served with roast garlic tomatoes, sautéd wild greens and home-made chutney. This mix freezes well.

Quince (*Cydonia oblonga*)

This is the true quince (as opposed to the flowering quince fruits, *Chaenomeles* spp.), and is widely grown in many parts of the world. In warmer climes the fruits can fully ripen and become sweet, but in the UK this rarely happens and we use the fruits in autumn, while still hard, in cooked recipes.

Quince makes a small tree, with beautiful white flowers in spring followed by apple- or pear-shaped fruits that ripen in late September/October. In humid climates such as the UK they can suffer badly from quince leaf blight, a fungal disease which can cause leaves to blacken and can completely defoliate the tree. There are some resistant varieties, so it is important to choose these if you are thinking of planting a tree.

Allow the fruits to remain on the tree for as long as possible before harvesting, then harvest carefully and store the fruits in a cool place – they should store for a few weeks.

Quinces are high in vitamin C, iron, potassium and copper. The fruits are hard when raw, but when cooked they have a soft, grainy texture (like some pears) and a beautiful delicate flavour with citrus and floral tones.

Quince & apple tart

Serves 4

6 medium quinces, peeled
2 medium cooking apples, peeled
About 2 tbsp Demerara sugar (to taste)
Lemon juice

Pastry:
115g (4oz) unsalted butter, at room temperature
50g (1¾oz) sugar
1 egg
200g (7oz) plain flour
Pinch of salt

Baking beans (dried beans or lentils)
A 25cm (10") flan dish

Preheat the oven to 180°C (350°F / Gas Mark 4)

Beat the butter and sugar with an electric whisk until smooth and creamy, then gently beat in the egg.

Sieve in the flour and salt to cover the mixture, then use your fingers to fold it in gently to form a doughy ball. It is important not to over-knead the pastry. Press it into a disc shape and put it in the fridge.

Roughly slice the apples and two of the quinces into a saucepan, discarding the cores, cover with water and sprinkle with the sugar. Put over a very low heat and cover with a lid. Simmer gently until the apples have become pulpy and the quince is soft. Cut the remaining quinces into quarters and core. Slice them lengthways to get long slices 3-5mm (up to ⅛") thick. Put in a bowl, cover with water and a little lemon juice and put to one side.

Grease the flan dish with a little butter and dust with flour. Take the pastry from the fridge and roll out on to a flour-dusted surface. Roll the pastry into a 30cm (12") circle. Pick the pastry up by rolling it on to your

rolling pin, lay it over the flan dish and press it gently into the sides of the dish. Slice off the excess with a knife. Place a layer of foil or baking parchment over the pastry and fill with baking beans to weight it. Prick the base with a fork to prevent air bubbles forming. Bake for 20 minutes.

Remove from the oven, remove the foil or parchment, and allow to cool. When the quinces and apples are soft, remove from the heat and strain off excess water. Mash into a rough purée and spread into the bottom of the flan dish. Now arrange your raw quince slices into two circles, as pictured above, slightly overlapping. Brush the top of the fruit and the pastry crust with some melted butter and bake for a further 20 minutes at 190°C (375°F / Gas Mark 5).

Slice and serve hot or cold with cream or yogurt.

Try this with pear and haws: the same quantity of pears as quinces in this recipe, and around 300g (10½oz) raw haws. Prepare the haws as for Haw & apple strudel (page 166) and add to stewed pears to spread on to the bottom of the pastry crust, then layer sliced pears on top.

186

Poached quinces with chestnuts & toffee medlars

Serves 4

4 large quinces

150ml (5¼fl oz) apple juice

70g (2½oz) caster sugar

¼ tsp ground cinnamon

¼ tsp ground nutmeg

4 cloves

200ml (7fl oz) water

2 tsp cornflour

100g (3½oz) toasted chestnuts, peeled and halved

8 toffee medlars (see recipe on page 178)

This recipe can be made with a slow cooker or on the hob in a large heavy-based saucepan. It will take around 1 hour 30 minutes in a slow cooker; 30 minutes on the hob. Preheat your slow cooker to 'Low'.

Put the apple juice, sugar, spices and half the water into a small saucepan and bring to the boil, stirring occasionally. Peel the quinces and cut into halves, removing the core with a teaspoon to leave a small oval cavity. When the syrup has come to the boil, turn it down to a low simmer. Stir the cornflour into the remaining water to form a smooth paste and slowly add to the syrup, stirring constantly until it thickens. Pour the syrup into the slow cooker or large saucepan and add the quinces and chestnuts, roll' and cover them with the syrup, and put on the lid.

Quinces are hard fruits and stay firm when cooked. Push in a fork, lift the quince from the pan and if it slides off it's done. If it sticks at all it needs longer.

With a slow cooker, check after 1 hour, taking care as a lot of steam may come out as you lift the lid. They

shouldn't take longer than 1 hour 30 minutes. On the hob, check after 20 minutes and make sure they are simmering gently. They shouldn't take longer than 40 minutes. When checking, you can spoon a little syrup over the tops of the fruits.

When the quinces are cooked, take them out of the syrup and place 2 halves on to each of 4 dessert plates. Place a medlar into each cavity and surround with chestnuts. Finish by spooning some of the spiced syrup over the fruits, and serve warm with cream or yogurt.

Try this with pears and walnuts using the same cooking times. You could also use wine or sherry instead of apple juice, as follows. Just bring the ingredients to the boil in a small pan, stirring continuously:

150ml (5¼fl oz) red wine or sherry

200ml (7fl oz) water

50g (1¾oz) brown sugar

Other recipes using quince: Baked American elderflower custard with flowering quince compote (page 110); Quince cheese (Part 1, page 22).

Sweet cicely (*Myrrhis odorata*)

Sweet cicely is a perennial herb growing about 60cm-1m (2-3') high. All parts of the plant are edible and have an excellent sweet anise flavour. The leaves can be used chopped in salads or, more traditionally, cooked with acid fruits such as apples or rhubarb, as they have a strong sweetening effect.

When green, sweet cicely seeds are quite sensational. Their flavour is incredibly sweet and similar to aniseed or liquorice, while their texture is crisp and succulent. This combination makes them irresistible to nibble on as a snack and they are so good on their own that they don't need anything else. However, if any do manage to make it through the kitchen door, they can really lift the flavour of salads, stir-fries and desserts.

The plant has a taproot that looks like a parsnip but, again, with an anise flavour. It can be used raw or cooked.

Sweet cicely contains useful amounts of vitamins A and C, calcium, iron, potassium and phosphorus.

Sweet cicely fruit salad

Serves 4

3 tbsp sweet cicely seeds
2 eating apples, cored and diced
200g (7oz) strawberries, hulled and halved
200g (7oz) blueberries
200g (7oz) fresh apricots, halved and pitted
300ml (10½fl oz) apple juice
2 tsp lemon juice
4 tbsp yogurt or cream

Place all of the fruit into a bowl along with the sweet
cicely seeds. Pour over the apple and lemon juice
and gently stir the ingredients together.

Serve with either yogurt or cream.

Other recipes using sweet cicely: Bamboo shoot yum (page 64); Stir-fried Good King Henry (page 78); Ice plant with
peanuts and coconut (page 86); Orpine & tomato salad (page 90); Spiced rhubarb fool (page 99); Plantain & sweet
cicely soup (page 134); Warm Turkish rocket & lentil salad (page 144).

Szechuan pepper
(*Zanthoxylum schinifolium*)

All members of this genus can be used as spices, but this one is particularly good. It forms a large rounded shrub, and is one of several *Zanthoxylum* species that have the name 'Szechuan pepper' attached to them. The leaves and fruits of this species have a wonderful citrus fragrance to them.

The leaves are used for flavouring, especially when young. The main crop, though, is the fruits – or, to be specific, the dried fruit 'shells' surrounding the black seeds. When the fruits ripen in September, the 'shells' turn red and split, revealing the seed within. The whole lot is then harvested, and the seeds optionally separated (they are tasteless). They need a little drying in our climate to store well. The spicy red shells are peppery and aromatic, like the leaves, and can be used directly in cooking, or ground as a spice.

The peppers are rich in essential oils (notably terpenes, which give the citrus flavours), and like black peppers they aid digestion. Note that most pepper mills do not grind the thin papery shells very efficiently; they can sometimes need shaking between grinding, or you can use a pestle and mortar.

Szechuan pepper is often used in China in the form of flavoured salt: toast or dry-fry equal amounts of coarse salt and peppercorns until the mixture just starts to smoke. When the mix is cool, grind to reduce to a coarse powder and use instead of salt and pepper. This is excellent on almost everything and Mark Diacono particularly recommends it on chips!

Chinese five-spice powder is frequently used in Szechuan cooking, especially with chicken, duck, pork and goose. It is a mixture of star anise, fennel, cinnamon, Szechuan peppercorns and cloves, toasted for a few minutes then ground to a powder. It is usually used either as a spice rub on the meat or is added to the breading for fried foods.

Szechuan chicken

One traditional use of this spice in China is to rub it on to meat (usually chicken or pork) before roasting.

225g (8 oz) chicken breast
1 tsp Szechuan peppercorns

Preheat the oven to 180°C (350°F / Gas Mark 4)

Roughly grind the peppercorns in a pestle and mortar (or use the end of rolling pin in a bowl). Place the chicken breasts on a foil-lined baking tray and rub the ground pepper thickly on to the upper surface. Wrap the foil around the chicken and place in the oven. After 30 minutes unwrap the foil from the top surface of the chicken and return to the oven for 15 minutes. Serve.

Other recipes using Szechuan pepper: Chinese artichoke stir-fry (page 199); Szechuan-infused rice vinegar (Part 1, page 26).

Szechuan & shiitake stir-fry

This Chinese-style dish comprises shiitake and oyster mushrooms in a simple aromatic marinade made with fresh Szechuan peppercorns, stir-fried with seasonal greens and walnuts.

Serves 4

2 tbsp fresh Szechuan peppercorns
150ml (5¼fl oz) boiling water
3 tsp honey
3 dsp soy sauce or tamari
10 fresh lemon balm leaves
150g (5¼oz) shiitake mushrooms, sliced
150g (5¼oz) oyster mushrooms, sliced lengthways
2 heaped tbsp welsh or spring onions, finely chopped
300g (10½oz) seasonal greens, shredded
100g (3½oz) walnut halves
2 tbsp vegetable oil

Place the Szechuan peppercorns into a bowl and gently bruise them with the back of a wooden spoon. You will hear them crack as you do so, and shiny black seeds will emerge from the red fleshy casing, releasing a lovely aroma. Add the boiling water, honey and soy sauce. Tear the lemon balm leaves and add them too, stirring all the ingredients together until the honey has dissolved. Cover the dish with a tea cloth and leave to stand for at least 20 minutes.

Next, strain the marinade through a sieve into a large bowl. Add the mushrooms to the marinade, turning them in until completely covered. The mushrooms will absorb the flavours and release them when cooked. Cover with a tea cloth and leave to marinate for 20 minutes.

Add the onions, greens and walnuts to the marinade. Put a wok on to a high heat and pour in the vegetable oil. When the oil is hot, add your mixed ingredients and stir. Stir-fry on a high heat for about 8 minutes, or until the vegetables are at your preferred softness. Ideally the greens should not wilt too much, but just soften to an emerald green colour. Stir continuously, ensuring the sauce has covered all of the ingredients.

Serve straight from the wok on to rice or noodles.

Try this with chicken or tofu. Cut two chicken breasts or a 255g (9oz) block of fresh tofu into long strips. Marinate in the Szechuan marinade with 150g (5¼oz) mushrooms for at least 1 hour, or preferably all day in the fridge. Heat the oil in a wok, remove the chicken or tofu from the marinade and stir-fry on a high heat for 3 minutes before adding the other vegetables.

 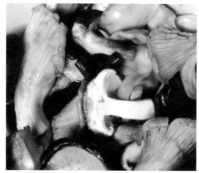 

Walnut (*Juglans regia*)

Walnut trees usually get very large with age; however, good varieties start producing nuts about 4-5 years from planting.

In the UK climate, fresh walnuts still contain a fair amount of water when ripe, and should be used within about 1 week, otherwise moulds will start to form on the outside on the nuts. To store properly they need drying, and usually (because this is in mid- or late October) artificial heat of some sort is needed to achieve proper dryness.

Walnuts are high in healthy fats (oils), protein, calcium, iron and numerous other minerals and vitamins. There are many recent medicinal studies showing the health benefits, particularly cardiovascular, of eating walnuts.

The nuts are borne within green husks that split on ripening to drop clean nuts to the ground. Cracking walnuts is fine by hand if you only have a few to do, but more than that and it becomes a chore. Some people build powered nut-cracking machines, but you can also buy a great hand-operated nut-cracking machine made in the USA (see Resources section).

Forest garden nut roast

Serves 4

200g (7oz) walnuts and chestnuts, shelled, toasted and chopped

170g (6oz) red lentils

485ml (17fl oz) veg stock

1 tbsp olive oil

100g (3½oz) onion, finely chopped

100g (3½oz) shiitake mushrooms, finely chopped

3 tsp ramsons pesto (see recipe on page 96)

2 eggs, beaten

150g (5¼oz) leftover cooked grain, e.g. brown rice or couscous

Freshly chopped thyme to taste

Salt and pepper

Garnish:

Walnut halves

A 1.5l (2¾ pint / 55fl oz) loaf tin

Preheat the oven to 190°C (375°F, Gas Mark 5)

Rinse the red lentils and cook in the vegetable stock in a covered saucepan for 15 minutes until all the stock is absorbed. Put the olive oil into a frying pan and fry the onions and mushrooms until they are soft, then stir in the pesto and cook for 1 minute.

Add the fried onions, mushrooms, eggs, cooked grain, thyme and chopped nuts to the lentils and stir together well. Add salt and pepper to taste. Oil the loaf tin and transfer your mixture to it, pushing it into the corners and levelling the top. Run a fork across the top to give some texture, brush with a little olive oil and garnish with walnut halves.

Cover the tin with foil and bake for 30 minutes, then remove the foil and bake for another 20 minutes. Remove from the oven and allow to rest for 5 minutes before cutting thick slices from the tin to serve with vegetables and gravy.

Walnuts are, of course, a fantastic food just eaten raw – try adding them to muesli for breakfast.

Other recipes using walnuts: Rhubarb & beetroot salad (page 96); Medlar & walnut slices (page 177); Crunchy yacon salad (page 223).

Winter

Babington's leek
(*Allium ampeloprasum* var. *Babingtonii*)

Also known as perennial leek

Babington's leek is one form of perennial leek (there are a few others). In the summer after flowering, it forms a head of bulbils (like small cloves of garlic) rather than seed, and dies back to a bulb underground for about 2 months before regrowing in the autumn.

The flavour of Babington's leek is more garlicky than the traditional annual-grown leek. No nutritional studies have been done on this plant, but undoubtedly it contains similar compounds to all the other alliums, which are antibacterial and antifungal.

Although you can cut the 'leek' stem off to harvest, when the plant will usually regrow, you can also pull or dig up whole plants, which gives much longer white stems. Although this may seem contradictory for a perennial plant, the fact is that this is such an easy plant to grow – just broadcast bulbils where you want it – that, once established, there are plenty of spare plants to harvest. Harvest plants between autumn and mid-spring, before they go to flower.

Babington's leek & potato bake

Serves 4

200g (7oz) Babington's leeks

25g (1oz) butter

1.4kg (3lb 3oz) potatoes, sliced into 5mm (⅛") rounds

70g (2½oz) grated Cheddar cheese

400ml (14fl oz) milk

55ml (2fl oz) vegetable stock

2 tsp Dijon mustard

Salt and pepper

4 eggs

A 25 x 25cm (10" x 10") lasagne dish

Preheat the oven to 170°C (325°F, Gas Mark 3)

Remove the soft bulb and tougher green leaves of the leeks and slice the white stems finely into rounds.

Sauté the leeks in butter for about 5 minutes. Place a single layer of the potato slices over the bottom of the lasagne dish, then layer alternately with a sprinkling of cheese and leeks. Top with a few leeks and a generous layer of cheese.

Put the milk, stock, mustard and seasoning into a bowl or jug and crack in the eggs. Whisk well and pour evenly over the layered vegetables.

Cover the dish with foil and bake for 45 minutes. Use a knife to check whether the potatoes are cooked. If they are still at all hard, replace the foil and cook until they are completely soft. Remove the foil and bake at 350°F (180°C / Gas Mark 4) for a further 10 minutes until browned.

Serve with fish or red meat and seasonal greens.

Other recipes using Babington's leek: Alexanders & Babington's leek linguine (page 57); Spicy alexanders and tomato soup (page 58).

Chinese artichoke
(*Stachys affinis*)

Chinese artichokes are sometimes called 'Crosnes', after the place in France where they were first grown in Europe. Related to woundwort (*Stachys officinalis*) and resembling it in growth, they have long been an important vegetable crop in China.

The tubers are very distinctive, white and cylindrical. Their flavour is mild (resembling a nutty Jerusalem artichoke) and they have a good crunchy texture. They are dug through the winter and are best left stored in the ground. Once harvested and in air they will store for about 1 week, but not much longer. They aren't huge but the harvest is pretty good and it is a very easy crop to grow, taking little effort.

Cleaning the tubers is easy: just soak them in water for 20 minutes, then agitate and give a final rinse in clean water.

100g (3½oz) of tubers contains around 20g (¾oz) of carbohydrate and 3g (⅛oz) of protein. Most of the rest of the content is water.

Chinese artichoke stir-fry

Serves 4

200g (7oz) Chinese artichokes

255g (9oz) tofu

1 tbsp honey

1 tbsp sesame seeds

3 tbsp soy sauce

800g (1lb 12oz) mixed vegetables, cut into long thin strips

2 garlic cloves, finely grated

5cm (2") cube fresh ginger, finely grated

1 tbsp sweet chilli sauce

75ml (2½fl oz) vegetable stock

2 tbsp sesame oil

2 tsp Chinese five spice

½ tsp ground Szechuan pepper

Preheat the oven to 150°C (300°F, Gas Mark 2)

Chop the tofu into 2.5cm (1") cube chunks and place into a spacious mixing bowl. Add the honey, sesame seeds and 1 tbsp soy sauce and stir together until evenly covered, taking care not to crumble the tofu. Transfer to a baking tray and bake for 25 minutes until browned.

Put all the vegetables into a large mixing bowl with the garlic and ginger and pour over the remaining 2 tbsp soy sauce, the sweet chilli sauce and the vegetable stock. Mix the ingredients well and ensure they are evenly coated with liquid.

Heat the sesame oil in a large wok over a high heat. Add the five spice and Szechuan pepper followed by all the other ingredients and stir-fry on a high heat for 10 minutes, or until the vegetables begin to soften. Test one of the harder vegetables, like carrot, and when they bend a little but still have crunch, the stir-fry is ready.

Serve on a bed of noodles or rice, with the tofu cubes on top of, or stirred into, the vegetables.

Try this without tofu, and instead bake the Chinese artichokes rather than adding them to the vegetables. Coat them in the honey, soy and sesame seeds and roast them at 180°C (350°F / Gas Mark 4) for 15 minutes or until soft and crispy. Cashews or other nuts can be added to the vegetable stir-fry, for protein.

Chinese artichoke & red onion pakoras

Pakoras are a traditional Indian snack of sliced vegetables deep-fried in a light, spiced batter. Chinese artichokes have a delicate, fragrant flavour and a light, crunchy texture which makes them ideal snacks. It is important to keep the batter fairly thin to avoid smothering the artichokes, so the consistency should be that of a thin pancake mix, but no thicker.

Serves 4-6

300g (10½oz) Chinese artichokes
255g (9oz) plain flour or gram flour
½ tsp baking powder
½ tsp chilli powder
1 tsp garam masala
1 tbsp lemon juice
2 tbsp chopped fresh coriander leaves
1 large red onion, halved and sliced
1 tsp salt
Vegetable oil as required

Sift and combine the flour, baking powder and spices into a large mixing bowl. Make a hole in the centre of the flour and into it add the lemon juice, then gradually whisk in small amounts of cold water. Do this slowly to ensure a smooth batter with no lumps. When you have achieved the consistency of a thin pancake mix, stop adding water and stir in the chopped coriander leaves and salt. Add the vegetables to the batter and stir in until well covered.

Pour a depth of around 5cm (2") of vegetable oil into a deep, heavy-based saucepan and put on to a medium heat, watching at all times, until hot. To gauge when the oil is up to temperature, take a little batter on a teaspoon and pour a drop into the pan. If it sizzles and quickly turns golden, the oil is ready. Reduce to a low heat and begin cooking. You may need to alter the heat as you cook, as you will need to fry the pakoras in batches, so the oil will cool down. Avoid the oil becoming too hot: you do not want the oil itself to boil, as this can become dangerous.

Using a large spoon, take a spoonful of pakora mixture at a time and drop into the hot oil. Depending on the size of your pan, you can do batches of several spoonfuls at a time. Watch each pakora and turn it in the oil so that it has an even colour. When the pakora is golden brown, remove it from the pan and lay it on some kitchen paper or newspaper to soak up the excess oil. You can keep each batch warm in the oven while you cook the rest, or you can take them straight to the table – they will be devoured by the time the next batch appears!

Serve hot or warm with sweet chutney and plain yogurt.

Try this with other forest garden vegetables, such as oca, Solomon's seal, ostrich fern shoots and slices of yam. Slice any combination of vegetables into thin strips and cook as above.

You can also add more spices to the batter if you like a stronger flavour. Yellow mustard seeds and whole cumin seeds work well, and you can increase the amount of chilli powder to your taste. For a real kick, add whole fresh chillies to the mix.

Egyptian onion
(*Allium cepa* Proliferum Group)

Also known as tree onion; walking onion

This plant, like several *Allium* species, produces bulbils (small aerial bulbs) on its stems instead of seeds. Sometimes it even makes bulbils which themselves start growing on the plant and produce their own bulbils. In this way it 'walks' about as the stems get weighed down and touch the ground where bulbils can root.

All parts have a sweet, mild onion flavour, and nutritionally will be very similar to onions, which are high in iron, manganese, potassium and vitamins B6 and C.

Unlike the common culinary onion, Egyptian onions remain perennial for many years. Although the bulbs can be eaten, the main crop is the green tubular leaves, which can be harvested at any time in the growing season (all year round in mild climates). The thicker stems nearer the ground can also be harvested in spring. The bulbils can be eaten too; they are best when young and do not need peeling.

Egyptian onion & smoked mackerel fishcakes

Serves 4

6-8 Egyptian onion leaves, chopped

255g (9oz) potatoes, diced into 2.5cm (1") cubes

Salt and pepper

55ml (2fl oz) single cream

1 tbsp lemon juice

30g (1oz) butter

200g (7oz) smoked mackerel fillets

80g (2¾oz) plain flour

2 eggs, beaten

100g (3½oz) breadcrumbs, made from fresh or stale bread

Vegetable oil

Place the potatoes into a saucepan, cover with boiling water, add a pinch of salt and boil for 8-10 minutes until soft. Strain and remove from the heat.

Add more salt and some ground black pepper to the potatoes along with the cream, lemon juice and butter. Mash the potatoes to a texture that is smooth but still has some small chunks. Remove the skin from the mackerel and break into small pieces, then add to the potato with the Egyptian onions. Mix the ingredients together thoroughly with a spoon until they are evenly distributed. Put the mixture into the fridge to cool for about 20 minutes.

Remove from the fridge and divide the mixture into 4 large or 8 small fishcakes, as you prefer, and roll into balls. Season the flour and put into one shallow dish, the beaten eggs into another and lay the bread-crumbs out over a chopping board. Roll each ball into the flour, then the egg, then the breadcrumbs, ensuring the whole surface is well covered. Finally flatten each ball into a cake shape and put aside.

Heat around 5cm (2") of vegetable oil in a spacious saucepan. Check the oil is up to heat by dropping in a few breadcrumbs. If they sizzle immediately the oil is hot enough; reduce the heat a little to prevent it from boiling. Carefully place each fishcake into the oil and fry for 2 minutes on each side, or until golden and crisp. Remove from the pan and place on to kitchen paper or newspaper to soak up excess oil.

The fishcakes can be served immediately, or chilled and then baked in the oven at a later time. If baking, place on a tray in the centre of an oven preheated to 160°C (320°F / Gas Mark 2½) and cook for 25 minutes. This can make the fishcakes crisper, and some people always bake their fishcakes after frying them.

The sweet flavour of Egyptian onion leaves makes them especially suitable for using in salads, sandwiches, etc.

Other recipes using Egyptian onion: Solomon's seal & Egyptian onion tart (page 101); Solomon's seal gnocchi (page 102).

Groundnut (*Apios americana*)

Groundnut is a perennial climber of the legume family from North America. It twines in the same way as runner beans, climbing up to about 3m (10'), and bears flowers which attract bees. Note that peanut is also sometimes called groundnut.

Each plant forms a large number of tubers, linked together by stringy root growth, and growing outwards from the centre of the plant. The tubers themselves vary in size and can reach 5cm (2") in diameter, but most are smaller. Some better selections have been made and yield many tubers of 2.5cm (1") diameter or more.

Long harvested by Native Americans, the starchy tubers were one of the crops that helped keep the first European settlers alive in their early years on the American continent.

The tubers are round or oval in shape and easy to clean. They are very high in protein – around 16 per cent – and high in carbohydrates.

The tubers are harvested from late autumn to spring (plants do not start growth very early in spring). Once you find some tubers you can follow the stringy roots to lift others.

Groundnut Röstis

Serves 4

300g (10½oz) groundnut, grated
1 medium red onion, finely sliced
2 eggs
Salt and pepper
3 tbsp flour
Vegetable oil

Place the groundnut, onion, eggs, salt and pepper into a mixing bowl and mix thoroughly. Sprinkle flour over the mixture a little at a time and stir in to cover and bind the ingredients.

Heat a little vegetable oil in a frying pan and add the mixture in small handfuls, flattening each one with the back of your spatula. Fry for about 4 minutes on each side over a medium heat, and keep turning until each side is golden brown and crispy.

Serve hot with greens and sausages or have them for breakfast with bacon.

Try this with other root vegetables and tubers. Potatoes, parsnips, ocas and yams work well in combination or on their own.

For a fresher taste, you could add a handful of chopped alexanders or coriander leaves to the mix.

You can spice up Röstis, too: add half a teaspoon of cumin seeds and half a teaspoon of mustard seeds.

Mediterranean groundnut stew

Serves 4

300g (10½oz) groundnut, diced

2 tbsp olive or vegetable oil

1 red onion, diced

150g (5¼oz) celery (including some leaves), chopped

3 garlic cloves, finely chopped

150g (5¼oz) carrots, diced

85g (3oz) whole black olives

2 tbsp paprika

¼ tsp cinnamon

2 tsp sugar

1 400g (14oz) tin tomatoes

1 tbsp tomato purée

1 400g (14oz) tin butter beans

1 tsp dried thyme

2 bay leaves

100ml (3½fl oz) vegetable stock

Salt and pepper

Preheat the oven to 170°C (325°F / Gas Mark 3)

In a heavy-based saucepan, heat a little olive or vegetable oil, add the onion and celery, and gently fry on a medium heat for 5 minutes. Add the garlic, groundnut, carrots, olives, paprika, cinnamon and sugar. Stir and fry for a further 2 minutes. Add the tomatoes, tomato purée, butter beans, herbs, stock

and seasoning, turn up the heat and bring to the boil. Transfer to a large, pre-warmed casserole dish and place in the centre of the oven for 50 minutes.

Take out of the oven and remove the lid, taking care to avoid the escaping steam. Use a sharp knife to check that the carrots and groundnut are soft – they should slide from the blade when it is inserted into them. If the vegetables are not cooked enough, replace the lid and return to the oven for at least a further 20 minutes and then check again.

Serve with rice or potatoes.

Mashua (*Tropaeolum tuberosum*)

Mashua is a climbing perennial used as a major root crop in the Andean region of South America. It is also called tuberous nasturtium, and is closely related to annual nasturtiums.

The stems clamber over supports or through bushes to reach about 2m (6'6') high each year. The leaves can be eaten (they have a similar peppery taste to annual nasturtiums), as can the orange flowers, although these are only produced from late autumn onwards.

Mashua tubers have a very distinctive flavour, which could be described as peppery, aniseed, bitter and sweet. The flavours alter depending on how they are cooked and what they are cooked with, but it's important to get accompanying flavours right so they are complementary. Gentle, sweet flavours seem to work best; strong, sour or bitter flavours such as cheese or vinegar seem to bring out the worst in them, but they sit well with other seasonal roots and tubers as well as pumpkins and squashes. When the combination is right, mashua is a delicious addition to the midwinter vegetable store.

Each plant forms a cluster of underground tubers, potato-sized but more cylindrical in shape. These can be harvested over the winter. Mashua contains about 80 per cent carbohydrate and 14-16 per cent protein. It is also high in vitamin C.

Mashua fried rice with bacon & beans

Serves 4

500g (1lb 1¾oz) mashua roots, cut into small chunks

300g (10½oz) short-grain brown rice or Arborio rice

255g (9oz) Brussels sprouts, peeled and halved

30g (1oz) butter

2 tbsp olive oil

6 rashers smoked back bacon, de-rinded and chopped into small pieces

4 spring onions, chopped into small rounds

2 garlic cloves, finely chopped

4 tbsp pine nuts

1 400g (14oz) tin mixed beans or 225g (8oz) mixed dried beans, cooked (after weighing)

2 tsp dried tarragon

Salt and pepper

Cook the rice according to instructions on the packet, and put to one side. Place the mashua and sprouts into a saucepan of boiling water with a pinch of salt. Boil for 6 minutes, strain and put to one side. Strain and rinse the beans and add them to the rice.

On a medium heat, melt the butter in a large heavy-based frying pan and add the olive oil. When the butter begins to sizzle, add the bacon, onions, garlic, pine nuts, mashuas and sprouts, and stir-fry for 5-10 minutes, or until the bacon is beginning to crisp and the vegetables are slightly browned. Add the rice, beans and tarragon to the frying pan and stir-fry for another 5 minutes or until the rice is heated through. Season well and serve straight away.

A mash of 1 part potato, 1 part swede and 2 parts mashua is truly delicious. Boil the swede and potato for 6 minutes, then add the mashua for a further 6 minutes. Mashua roasts and bakes well, too.

Other recipes using mashua: Oca, coconut & red lentil curry (page 211).

Oca (*Oxalis tuberosa*)

Oca is a bushy perennial plant growing about 30cm (1') high, related to wood sorrel and with leaves that look very similar.

It is a staple vegetable in South America and is now growing in popularity in the UK and elsewhere. This is testament to its flavour, versatility and beautiful appearance. Oca tubers have a lemon-like flavour that is intense and acidic when first harvested, but which mellows and sweetens over time as they ripen. Eaten raw, they have a wonderful crunchy texture and a creamy, lemon-balm taste, which makes them great in salads, where their bright skins can be fully appreciated. They can also be enjoyed just as they come, as a fruit-like winter snack. The flavour is more subtle when cooked, but still distinctive, and oca is great roasted, steamed, sautéd and added to casseroles, stews and curries.

Oca is high in vitamin C, potassium and phosphorus.

Mexican oca salad

A common way to eat oca in Mexico is as a simple salad of raw oca, lemon juice, chilli and salt. Here is a salad based on this simple combination, with a few irresistible additions.

Serves 4

500g (1lb 1¾oz) oca tubers, sliced into 4mm (⅛") rounds

Half a lime, juice and zest

2 tbsp fresh chopped coriander leaves

85g (3oz) pitted black olives

Large handful of sprouted seeds (alfalfa or cress)

2 tbsp olive oil

½ tsp cayenne pepper

Salt and black pepper

Place the oca into a spacious salad bowl with the lime juice and zest. Add all the other ingredients, toss together thoroughly and taste. You can tweak the quantities of ingredients according to your preference.

This salad is a great accompaniment to Mexican dishes, especially with some soured cream or guacamole.

Try oca roasted in olive oil with thyme, salt and black pepper.

Sadly the bright colours fade a little with cooking, but they are still an attractive side vegetable. Oca is also delicious mashed with butter, cream and dill, or simply steamed for 8-10 minutes and rolled in a little olive oil and salt.

Oca, coconut & red lentil curry

Oca's citrus flavour works well with aromatic spices and rich, sweet coconut. This light yet filling recipe brings these elements together in a simple, tasty main dish.

Serves 4

350g (12¼oz) oca tubers, cut into bite-sized chunks

2 medium onions, diced

2 medium leeks, sliced into 1cm (⅜") rounds

Sunflower oil

2 garlic cloves, peeled and crushed

5cm (2") piece fresh ginger, peeled and finely grated

½ tsp chilli powder

2 tsp ground coriander

1 tsp ground cumin

Small bunch of coriander

1l (1¾ pints / 35fl oz) vegetable stock

200g (7oz) red split lentils

2 star anise

Juice of half a lime

200g (7oz) carrots, diced

200ml (7fl oz) boiling water

100g (3½oz) creamed coconut (from a block)

150g (5¼oz) mashua tubers, cut into bite-sized chunks

Salt

Garnish:
Coriander leaves

Place the onions and leeks into a large saucepan and fry on a medium heat for 5 minutes in plenty of sunflower oil. Add the garlic and ginger to the pan along with the chilli, ground coriander and ground cumin. Continue to fry gently for a further 3 minutes, ensuring that you don't burn the spices and that you have enough oil to prevent them from sticking to the pan. Take the fresh coriander, finely chop the stalks and add them to your vegetable stock. Coarsely chop the leaves and put them to one side.

Add the lentils, star anise, lime juice and vegetable stock to the pan, cover, bring to the boil and simmer on a low heat for 10 minutes. Then add the carrots, replace the lid, and cook for a further 5 minutes.

Pour the boiling water into a jug and chop the creamed coconut into small chunks. Add the coconut to the water and stir it until it has dissolved. Add the coconut water, mashua, oca and half of the coriander leaves to the pan and simmer for a further 6-10 minutes until the oca are soft. Overcooking will make the oca and mashua soft and mushy, so if you prefer a bit of crunch in the oca to give more texture to the dish, keep a close check on them for the last few minutes of cooking. Add salt to taste and remove from the heat.

Serve with rice and sprinkle with the remaining coriander leaves.

Shiitake (*Lentinula edodes*)

Shiitake are one of several mushrooms suitable for growing as crops in forest gardens, and are usually grown on logs. But shiitake have an advantage over most other log fungi crops in that they are more easily forced into cropping and therefore more controllable. Shiitake logs are 'shocked' – a combination of soaking and hitting – which makes them produce mushrooms 1-2 weeks later.

Other mushrooms can of course be grown on logs, the most notable being oyster mushrooms, but none seem as controllable as shiitake. With these others you have to wait until weather conditions stimulate mushroom production, usually in late autumn.

After shocking, the first sign of a crop of mushrooms is tiny 'buds' which appear across the log. These rapidly grow and form mushrooms which enlarge, the caps flattening out as they mature. Harvest before they 'go over' (at that stage you will find mushroom flies in them!) by twisting them off the log.

The stalks of shiitake are tough and inedible, so these are cut off and only the caps are used. Shiitake mushrooms are high in many minerals, and also in vitamin B6, Riboflavin and Niacin.

Shiitake & pork stew

Serves 4

200g (7oz) shiitake mushrooms

2 tbsp vegetable oil

500g (1lb 1¾oz) pork, diced

1 onion, diced

2 celery sticks, chopped

1 large carrot, chopped into rounds

1 tbsp plain flour

500ml (18fl oz) chicken stock

150ml (5¼fl oz) red wine

½ tbsp chopped fresh rosemary

½ tbsp chopped fresh sage

Salt and pepper

Pour the vegetable oil into a large, heavy-based saucepan and place over a medium heat. Add the pork and sear for 5 minutes, sealing all sides.

Add the onion, celery and carrots to the pork and fry for a further 2 minutes. Turn off the heat and add the flour, stirring to cover the ingredients in the pan and absorb the oil. Slowly add the stock, stirring continuously to combine with the flour and oil. Add the wine, herbs, salt and pepper.

Bring to the boil and reduce to low heat. Simmer for 50-60 minutes until the pork is tender. Serve with rice or potatoes.

Shiitake risotto

Serves 4

200g (7oz) shiitake mushrooms, sliced

30g (1oz) butter

1 tbsp olive oil

1 onion, diced

2 garlic cloves, finely chopped

400g (14oz) risotto rice

200ml (7fl oz) dry white wine

1.7l (3 pints / 60fl oz) vegetable or chicken stock

4 tbsp chopped fresh basil

70g (2½oz) grated Parmesan

Salt and pepper

Garnish:

2 tbsp toasted pine nuts

Melt the butter and olive oil in a saucepan and add the onions. Fry over a medium heat for 3 minutes,

then add the mushrooms and fry for a further 3 minutes. Add the garlic and fry for 1 minute more. Add the rice and wine and cook for 2 minutes, stirring continuously.

Add the stock and half of the fresh basil to the pan and stir. Bring to the boil and reduce to a low heat. Cover and simmer for 20 minutes, stirring occasionally, then taste the rice to test the texture. It's important not to cook the rice for too long, as it becomes stodgy. It is best that the rice is al dente; cooked through with a little bite. Add more water if the risotto becomes dry and the rice needs more cooking time.

When you are satisfied with the rice, remove from the heat and add the Parmesan, remaining basil, and salt and pepper to taste. Stir together well and serve with a sprinkling of toasted pine nuts.

Other recipes using shiitake: Forest garden nut roast (page 194); Chinese yacon with cashews (page 222).

Siberian purslane
(*Claytonia sibirica*)

Siberian purslane is a low-growing woodland perennial, naturalised all over Europe, with bright green foliage; it is evergreen in mild locations.

This is a great early salad crop with a delicate flavour and succulent texture, making it an ideal base for leaf salads. The stems, leaves and flowers are all edible and when eaten raw have a beet-like flavour, sweet and fresh with a very slight bitterness. Crucially, unlike many other perennial salads, it does not have a strong or hot taste. When cooked it is very similar to spinach in taste, texture and appearance, and is delicious wilted with butter or added to soups and sauces.

Claytonia species are a good source of vitamin C and are unusually high in omega-3 fatty acids.

Purslane penne

Serves 4

200g (7oz) Siberian purslane

1 medium onion, sliced

Olive oil

2 tsp brown sugar

2 garlic cloves, finely sliced

1½ 400g (14oz) tins chopped plum tomatoes

1 tbsp tomato purée

200ml (7fl oz) vegetable stock

1 tin butter beans or haricot beans

Salt

400g (14oz) penne

2 tsp dried oregano or 1 tbsp chopped fresh oregano

70g (2½oz) Chèvre goat's cheese, chopped into chunks

Preheat the oven to 200°C (400°F / Gas Mark 6)

In a large, deep saucepan fry the onions in plenty of olive oil with the sugar until soft. Add the garlic and fry for 1 more minute. Add the tomatoes, tomato purée, vegetable stock and butter beans and bring to the boil. Simmer gently while you prepare the pasta.

Fill a deep saucepan with boiling water and add a good pinch of salt. Add the penne to the water and bring back to a rolling boil. Turn down to medium heat and cook according to the instructions on the packet. Remove from the heat, strain and transfer to a lasagne dish. Drizzle over a little olive oil and salt and stir in, then cover with a clean tea towel.

Place all of the purslane and oregano into the pan of tomato sauce, cover and turn up the heat. Remove the lid after 1-2 minutes and the purslane will have wilted. Turn the heat down and stir the purslane into the sauce. Pour the sauce over the penne in the lasagne dish and scatter the chunks of goats' cheese over the top. Place the dish uncovered in the oven and bake for 15-20 minutes until the cheese begins to brown.

Remove from the oven and serve immediately with warm Italian ciabatta and olives.

Siberian purslane salad with ramsons & hazelnut dressing

Serves 4

100g (3½oz) purslane, roughly chopped
1 large carrot, peeled and grated
10g chopped fresh fennel leaves

Dressing:
3 large ramsons leaves
2 tbsp lemon juice
3 tbsp virgin olive oil
2 tbsp toasted hazelnuts
¼ tsp salt
½ tsp cracked black pepper

Stick blender

Place the purslane, carrot and fennel together in a salad bowl and toss until well mixed.

To make the dressing, put all the ingredients into a large jug and blend briefly with a stick blender so that the hazelnuts are chopped but not ground – this gives the salad some extra crunch.

If serving immediately, dress the salad and mix well. If you plan to eat later, the salad will keep fresher undressed until just before serving. You can tweak the ratios of the ingredients according to preference, and if your lemon juice is very tart you could add a teaspoon of honey before blending the dressing, to soften the flavour.

Try Siberian purslane wilted with a poached egg on top, plenty of salt and cracked pepper and some bread and butter. If you are feeling adventurous you could even venture to Hollandaise sauce for a forest garden 'Eggs Benedict'.

Skirret (*Sium sisarum*)

Skirret is one of those vegetables that was formerly widely grown but now is pretty much forgotten. It was grown by the Romans (and was a favourite of the Emperor Tiberius) and the Picts and its origins are unknown. It is a perennial plant of the umbellifer family, a little parsnip-like in appearance, with a cluster of pale finger-thick taproots.

It is best grown in a moist soil – in dry soils the roots can become woody. Plants are allowed to grow and flower – as with other umbellifers, the flowers are useful to attract beneficial insects.

Harvest roots in winter (leave stored in the ground if possible). Skirret roots have a flavour with elements of parsnip, carrot and liquorice. When preparing them, it reduces the scrubbing required if you soak them in water for 10-15 minutes beforehand. Skirret makes a great addition to stews, casseroles and soups, as well as being delicious when raw. The sweet, mellow and earthy flavour is perfect for comforting winter cooking, and the flavour, although similar to that of parsnip, is less overpowering.

Cheesy skirret bundles

Serves 4

20 skirret roots

3 large savoy cabbage leaves, sliced into long, 2.5cm (1")-wide strips, ribs removed

Cheese sauce:
50g (1¾oz) butter
50g (1¾oz) flour
500ml (18fl oz) milk
80g (2¾oz) cheese, grated
1 tsp wholegrain mustard

Preheat the oven to 200°C (400°F, Gas Mark 6)

Lay two or three of the cabbage strips on top of one another on a chopping board and place five pieces of skirret root on top of the strips. Wrap the cabbage around the skirret and secure with natural, undyed string. Repeat this to create four bundles and then transfer them to a steamer. Steam for 4 minutes and put aside while you make the cheese sauce.

Melt the butter over a low heat in a medium saucepan and when it has completely melted turn off the heat. Add the flour and whisk into a smooth paste. Gradually add the cold milk, whisking constantly until combined and smooth. Return to a medium heat, stirring constantly, and when the milk begins to steam, add half the cheese and the mustard. Turn down the heat if the sauce begins to bubble. When the cheese has fully combined, remove from the heat.

Place each bundle into a small ovenproof dish and pour a quarter of the sauce over each. Divide the remaining grated cheese on to each bundle and set the four dishes on to a baking tray. Place into the oven and bake for 10-15 minutes. Remove when the cheese is brown and bubbling, and serve immediately.

Try this with slices of carrot or spring onion added to the skirret. Serve as a starter or side dish, or wrap in ham, bake together in a lasagne dish and serve with baked potatoes.

Cream of skirret soup

This warming winter soup is delicate, earthy and very moreish!

Serves 4-6

300g (10½oz) skirret, chopped into 1cm (⅜") rounds

30g (1oz) butter

300g (10½oz) leeks, chopped into 1cm (⅜") rounds

70g (2½oz) celery, chopped

225g (8oz) potatoes, diced

1.2l (2 pints / 40fl oz) vegetable stock

150ml (5¼fl oz) double cream

Salt and pepper

Stick blender

Melt the butter in a saucepan and fry the leeks over a medium heat for 3 minutes. Add the skirret, celery and potatoes. Pour in the stock, bring to the boil and simmer for 10 minutes.

Blend with a stick blender until smooth, then stir in the cream, season to taste and serve.

Like other root vegetables, skirret lends itself well to stews, casseroles and soups, but can also be eaten raw. Roots can have a stringy core, which is fiddly to remove. When cooking, you can slice the roots into of 1cm (³/₈") rounds, which makes the stringy centre unnoticeable. If eating raw, you can remove the strings by snapping one end to reveal the string and then pull the string down along the length of the root and out at the other end. Another method is to slice the root lengthways and pull the strings out from one end to the other.

Combine thin strips of raw skirret with thin slices of celery, carrot and Chinese artichokes with seed sprouts and toasted pine nuts. Dress in a simple balsamic dressing and serve.

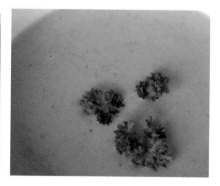

Yacon (*Smallianthus sonchifolia*)

Yacon is a tuber crop from South America, where it is highly valued. It becomes a large and sturdy plant, up to 2m (6'6") high, with huge felted leaves.

The round, potato-sized storage tubers are quite remarkable. If you scrub one clean then bite into it, the sensation is almost identical to that of biting into an Asian pear: it is very juicy, with a flowery fragrance and crisp texture. The tubers can be used raw in salads, or in cooked recipes, where the texture resembles water chestnut.

The tubers contain starch in the form of inulin (like Jerusulem artichokes), and if you are not used to eating them you might get some windy effects! These will reduce if you eat yacon regularly. Although you may not get much carbohydrate from the tubers, they are high in minerals and vitamins.

Yacon tubers are harvested in autumn after the first frosts, or through the winter in mild areas.

Chinese yacon with cashews

Serves 4

1 medium yacon, peeled and diced into 2.5cm (1") cubes

255g (9oz) carrot, cut into rounds

2 red peppers, cut into 2.5cm (1") squares

700ml (1¼ pints / 25fl oz) vegetable stock

2 tbsp sesame oil

1 leek, cut into rounds

3 spring onions, cut into rounds

1 celery stick, sliced

100g (3½oz) shiitake mushrooms, cut into halves

3 garlic cloves, crushed

25g (¾oz) fresh ginger, finely grated

½ dried chilli, finely chopped

2 tsp honey

3 tsp soy sauce

2 tbsp oyster sauce

100g (3½oz) cashews

Yacon is used in place of water chestnuts in this simple Chinese-style stew. Even when cooked the yacon retains its crisp, fresh flavour.

Place the yacon, carrots and peppers into a deep saucepan and cover all with the vegetable stock. Bring to the boil and simmer on a medium heat for 5 minutes. Pour the sesame oil into a non-stick frying pan or wok and place over a medium heat. Add the leeks, spring onions, celery, mushrooms, garlic and ginger, and fry gently for 3 minutes.

Take both pans off the heat and add the contents of the frying pan to those in the saucepan. Stir in the chilli, honey, soy sauce and oyster sauce, and return to a medium heat. Bring to the boil and simmer for a further 10 minutes, until all the vegetables are soft. While the stew is simmering place the cashews on to a baking tray and toast under a low grill for 3 minutes.

Remove the saucepan from the heat and stir in the cashews.

Serve with jasmine rice as a main, or as a chunky soup to warm you up on a chilly day.

Try yacon and cashews Thai-style using a curry paste and coconut milk: chop mushrooms, onions, red peppers and leeks, and fry in sesame oil for 3 minutes, then stir in paste (see jar for instructions on quantity) and fry for a further 3-5 minutes. Add diced yacon and sweet potato or squash and cover with coconut milk. Simmer for 20 minutes on a low heat. Toast cashews and add just before serving with white rice.

Both recipes also work well with diced chicken breast.

Crunchy yacon salad

Serves 4

1 medium yacon (approximately 300g/10½oz), peeled and sliced into matchsticks

1 large carrot, grated

A quarter of a medium red cabbage, shredded

1 celery stick, finely chopped

1 welsh onion leaf, finely chopped

50g (1¾oz) walnuts, roughly chopped

Dressing:

255g (9oz) yogurt

Half a lemon and finely grated zest

1 tbsp chopped fresh fennel leaf

Milk (if needed)

When combined with other seasonal vegetables, yacon adds a crisp freshness that really lifts a winter salad.

To make the dressing, put the yogurt into a spacious jug, add the rest of the ingredients and stir together. Yogurt varies in texture, so if necessary add a little milk to get a thick but runny consistency. Put aside while you make the salad.

Place all salad ingredients into a large mixing bowl and toss well. Spoon the salad on to plates and drizzle the dressing over it in stripes. Serve as a side salad, or alone with bread and butter.

Tip: make your dressing first, then the salad. The carrot, yacon and cabbage all dull soon after being chopped, so make the salad just before you want to serve it if possible. If you're not able to do this you could toss the salad in a little lemon juice and water, or you could add the dressing to the salad to make more of a slaw.

Yams (*Dioscorea* spp.)

Also known as air potatoes

Yams are an excellent perennial carbohydrate crop, and the hardier species (*D. batatas, D. japonica*) can be grown in the UK climate. They are twining climbers and produce numerous aerial tubers up the stems, as well as one or more large storage root tubers. Both types can be used. The aerial tubers have a similar texture and bite to the root tubers. They are chickpea-sized and, if you have a big enough crop, make a good home-grown substitute for chickpeas.

Yams are a staple carbohydrate in the Caribbean and are often eaten mashed as a side vegetable with meat dishes, or, as in the recipe opposite, in a curry or stew.

As well as being high in carbohydrates and fibre, yams are also high in vitamins C and B6, and in potassium, manganese and other minerals.

Harvest aerial tubers in late summer and autumn as the leaves start to turn yellow; it is useful to put down a sheet or blanket beneath plants as you harvest, as you are bound to knock some off. The ground tubers can be dug in winter after the plant has died down, and stored in dry earth, or (in mild regions) left in the ground until required.

Jamaican chicken curry with yams

The most common meats eaten in Jamaica are chicken, goat and codfish. Any of these work well in this recipe, although you may struggle to get hold of goat meat unless you rear them yourself!

Serves 4

Spice mix:

2 tsp allspice

1 tsp chilli powder

½ tsp dried thyme

½ tsp ground black pepper

1 tsp dried garlic

2 tsp paprika

1 tsp turmeric

3 bay leaves

3 tsp muscovado sugar

2 tbsp vegetable oil

500g (1lb 1¾oz) yam root tubers, peeled and diced into 2.5cm (1") cubes

2 tsp lemon juice

1 large onions, diced

3 medium bell peppers, diced

4 large chicken thighs

3 cloves fresh garlic

350ml (13fl oz) hot chicken stock

Sprig of fresh thyme

1 tsp salt

Preheat the oven to 150°C (300°F, Gas Mark 2)

Put all of the spices, bay leaves and sugar in a bowl with the oil and mix well. Add the garlic to the hot chicken stock and add the thyme, bay leaves and salt. Spread the spice mix over the chicken thighs and put to one side while you prepare the vegetables.

Place the yams into a bowl with the lemon juice sprinkled over. Place the onion and peppers into a large flying pan with the chicken thighs. Fry over a high heat until the chicken is sealed all over and the vegetables have browned.

Put the chicken, vegetables and yams into a deep baking dish with a lid. Add the garlic to the hot chicken stock and add the thyme and salt. Stir well and pour over the ingredients in the baking dish. Cover and place in the centre of the oven for 1 hour, or until the chicken juices run clear.

Serve with rice and greens.

Yam & coconut bake

Serves 4

400g (14oz) yam root tubers, sliced into thin rounds, approximately 4mm (⅛")

2 medium carrots, sliced into thin rounds, approximately 4mm (⅛")

1 medium red pepper, sliced into thin strips

1 medium red onion, finely sliced

100g (3½oz) creamed coconut (from a block)

300ml (10½fl oz) hot vegetable stock

3 garlic cloves, crushed

1 tsp allspice

1 tsp dried thyme

½ tsp chilli

½ tsp salt

Preheat the oven to 180°C (350°F / Gas Mark 4)

In a deep baking dish, place the slices of vegetables in alternate layers, finishing with a layer of yam slices. Chop the creamed coconut into small chunks and dissolve into the hot vegetable stock. Add the garlic, allspice, thyme, chilli and salt, and stir well. Pour the liquid over the layered vegetables and put a lid on the baking dish. Bake for 30 minutes covered, then remove the lid and bake for a further 20 minutes, or until the top has browned and crisped a little.

Serve with meat or roasted tofu and seasonal greens.

Try this recipe with a totally different flavour. Layer cheese between the vegetables, beat 4 eggs with 150ml (5¼fl oz) milk and add 2 crushed garlic cloves, some chopped fresh thyme, tarragon, salt and pepper. Pour the egg mix over the vegetables and bake as above.

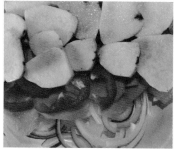

Moroccan-style aerial yams

Serves 4

150g (5¼oz) aerial yam tubers
1 medium red onion, diced
1 400g (14oz) tin chickpeas
Handful of chopped fresh coriander

Roasted vegetables (all chopped into bite-sized chunks):
2 large carrots
2 medium yam root tubers
2 medium fennel bulbs
1 medium sweet potato
Olive oil

Spice mix:
2 tsp paprika
1½ tsp brown sugar
1 tsp ground coriander
½ tsp ground cumin
½ tsp salt
½ tsp pepper
½ tsp fennel seeds
½ tsp ground ginger
¼ tsp chilli powder
¼ tsp cinnamon
¼ tsp cardamom
¼ tsp ground clove
3 tbsp olive oil

Tahini sauce:
6 tbsp tahini
2 garlic cloves, crushed
1 tbsp lemon juice
½ tsp salt
340ml (12fl oz) boiling water

Stick blender

Preheat the oven to 180°C (350°F / Gas Mark 4)

Put the vegetables for roasting into a large bowl with a glug of oil and roll them until they are well coated. Transfer to a baking tray and roast for 40 minutes or until soft, crisp and browned.

Grind the spices with a pestle and mortar until the fennel seeds are well crushed. Add the olive oil and mix to form a paste. Put the onion, yam and chickpeas in a large frying pan or wok. Add the spice paste and stir in evenly. Stir-fry on a medium heat for 10-15 minutes, until the onions are soft and the spice mix has formed a crisp caramelised coating over the chickpeas and yams.

To make the tahini sauce, put all ingredients into a jug and blend with a stick blender until smooth.

Add the roasted vegetables from the oven to the yams and chickpeas with the fresh coriander. Over a high heat, gently stir all ingredients together until heated through. Serve on a bed of couscous. Drizzle the tahini sauce over the top to finish.

Try aerial yams lightly toasted in a dry frying pan, or steamed and rolled in butter and salt.

Appendix 1: Forest garden food plants

This table lists all the edible plants from *Creating a Forest Garden* and gives cooking tips or references to them where they appear in this book.

Plant		Part	Cooking tips / page references
Alexanders (also known as black lovage)	*Smyrnium olusatrum*	Leaves/stems	See page 56.
		Seeds	Grind the seeds in a pepper mill or with a pestle and mortar. They have an intense alexanders flavour, excellent in soups, stews, etc.
		Roots	Use like other root vegetables, e.g. parsnips.
Alfalfa (also known as lucerne)	*Medicago sativa*	Shoots	The young 5cm (2") shoots can be used raw in salads or steamed/stir-fried in cooked dishes.
Almond	*Prunus dulcis*	Nuts	See page 39 (drying).
American allspices	*Calycanthus* spp.	Bark	Bark of 1-2cm (⅜-¾") branches is peeled off and dried, then used as you would cinnamon sticks.
American elder	*Sambucus canadensis*	Flowers	See page 108.
		Fruits	Fruits can be used in all the same ways as European elder – cooked and mixed with other fruits, made into wine, etc.
Anise hyssop	*Agastache foeniculum*	Leaves	Used as an aromatic herb, raw in salads or cooked in soups and other dishes – anise flavour.
Apple	*Malus domestica*	Fruits	See page 33 (drying) and page 38 (fruit leather).
Apple mint	*Mentha suaveolens*	Leaves/shoots	See page 60.
Apple rose (also known as rugosa rose)	*Rosa rugosa*	Flowers	Strong flavour; particularly good sprinkled on to summer salads.
		Fruits	See page 148.
Apricot	*Prunus armeniaca*	Fruits	See page 33 (drying).
Asian pear	*Pyrus pyrifolia* & *P. ussuriensis*	Fruits	Mostly used fresh. See page 34 (drying) and 38 (fruit leather).
Autumn olive	*Elaeagnus umbellata*	Fruits	See page 152 and page 38 (fruit leather).
Babington's leek (also known as perennial leek)	*Allium ampeloprasum* var. *babingtonii*	Bulbils	Used young before a papery surface layer develops; particularly good in stews.
		Stems/leaves	See page 196.
Bamboos	*Phyllostachys* spp., *Pleioblastus simonii*, *Pseudosasa japonica*, *Semiarundinaria fastuosa* and *Yushania* spp.	Shoots	See page 62.
Bay	*Laurus nobilis*	Leaves	Many well-known traditional uses.
Bayberries (also known as wax myrtles)	*Myrica* spp.	Leaves	Similar in flavour to true bay, and can be used in all the same ways, but does not dry so well.
Beech	*Fagus sylvatica*	Young leaves	See page 66.

Plant		Part	Cooking tips / page references
Bellflowers (also known as harebells)	*Campanula* spp.	Leaves/shoots	Best used in salads; quality varies between species.
		Flowers	Used in salads.
Bentham's cornel	*Cornus capitata*	Fruits	Pulp is eaten fresh – sweet, banana-flavoured; skins bitter. Pulp very good in fruit leathers.
Birches	*Betula* spp.	Sap	Tapped in late winter, can be drunk fresh (slightly sweet), otherwise best made into wine.
Bittercresses	*Cardamine flexuosa* & *C. hirsuta*	Leaves/shoots	All parts peppery and spice up salads. Also used like watercress in soups.
Blackberry	*Rubus fruticosus*	Fruits	Used fresh or cooked.
Blackcurrant	*Ribes nigrum*	Fruits	Eaten raw or cooked in many dishes. See page 37 (fruit leather).
		Leaves	Used for herb teas, but can also be used as a flavouring, for instance in ice cream and other desserts.
Blackthorn (also known as sloe)	*Prunus spinosa*	Fruits	Traditionally used in sloe gin, but if fruits are crushed and exposed to air and/or cooked the astringency is removed and then can be used in desserts, fruit leathers, etc.
Black walnut	*Juglans nigra*	Nuts	Use in all the same ways as walnut. See page 39 (drying).
Bladdernuts (European & American)	*Staphylea pinnata* & *S. trifolia*	Seeds	Eat raw after shelling – pistachio-flavoured.
Blue honeysuckle (also known as honeyberry)	*Lonicera caerulea*	Fruits	Eaten fresh.
Blue bean	*Decaisnea fargesii*	Pulp from pods	Eat raw out of pods. Also good in mixed fruit leathers after seeds have been removed.
Blueberries	*Vaccinium* spp.	Fruits	Mainly eaten raw or in desserts. See page 189 and page 38 (fruit leather).
Bog myrtle	*Myrica gale*	Leaves	Similar in flavour to true bay, and can be used in all the same ways, but does not dry so well.
Bowles's mint	*Mentha* Bowles's mint	Leaves/shoots	Mild mint, suitable for using in bulk amounts in salads and herb teas, or when lightly cooked.
Buartnut	*Juglans* x *bixbyi*	Nuts	Use in all the same ways as walnut.
Buffalo berries	*Shepherdia* spp.	Fruits	Astringent until fully ripe, then very nice raw, excellent in jams and fruit leathers.
Buffalo currant	*Ribes odoratum*	Fruits	Eaten raw, cooked or preserved like other currants.
Bullaces	*Prunus insititia*	Fruits	Use cooked as for damsons.
Burnets	*Sanguisorba* spp.	Leaves/shoots	Mild-flavoured, suitable for using in decent quantities in salads.
Butternut	*Juglans cinerea*	Nuts	Use in all the same ways as walnut.
California allspice	*Calycanthus occidentalis*	Bark	Bark of 1-2cm (⅜-¾") branches is peeled off and dried, then used as you would cinnamon sticks.
Cardoon	*Cynara cardunculus*	Flower buds	Use exactly as for globe artichoke.
		Leaf stalks	See page 111.
Caucasian spinach	*Hablitzia tamnoides*	Leaves/shoots	Use cooked lightly as a perennial spinach with an excellent flavour.

Plant		Part	Cooking tips / page references
Caucasian whortleberry	*Vaccinium arctostaphylos*	Fruits	Use like blueberries (to which they are closely related).
Cherry plum	*Prunus cerasifera*	Fruits	Mainly eaten raw. Also very useful in mixed fruit leathers as a sweetener.
Cherry (sour)	*Prunus cerasus*	Fruits	Normally cooked and sweetened in dessert dishes.
Cherry (sweet)	*Prunus avium*	Fruits	Mainly eaten raw. See page 38 (fruit leather).
Chestnuts	*Castanea* spp.	Nuts	See page 156 and page 40 (drying).
Chickweed	*Stellaria media*	Leaves/shoots	Mild-flavoured, suitable for using in good amounts in salads, or can be cooked lightly in stir-fries, etc.
Chicory	*Cichorium intybus*	Leaves/shoots	See page 115.
		Roots	These are harvested in autumn/winter and roasted then ground to make a powdered coffee-like drink.
Chilean guava	*Myrtus ugni*	Fruits	The delicious fruits are best eaten raw.
Chinese artichoke	*Stachys affinis*	Tubers	See page 198.
Chinese bramble (also known as groundcover raspberry)	*Rubus tricolor*	Fruits	Like raspberries, best eaten raw as they do not have a long shelf life after harvesting. Also in jams.
Chinese cedar (also known as toon)	*Toona sinensis*	Leaves/shoots	See page 67.
Chinese dogwood	*Cornus kousa*	Fruits	Eat fresh in late autumn when fully ripe and soft, or use pulp in desserts / fruit leathers. Pawpaw-flavoured.
Chinkapin	*Castanea pumila*	Nuts	Sweeter than chestnuts and good eaten raw. Also used in all the ways chestnuts are.
Chocolate vine	*Akebia quinata*	Pulp from pods	The pulp is nice eaten fresh, otherwise best used in mixed fruit leathers after seeds are removed.
Chokeberries (also known as aronia berries)	*Aronia* spp.	Fruits	Normally made into juice to mix with others, or cooked with other fruits. Also in mixed fruit leathers. Flavour when raw is mediocre but it is very high in vitamins.
Colewort	*Crambe cordifolia*	Leaves/shoots	Cook lightly like cabbage leaves.
		Flowering heads	Use like broccoli.
		Flowers	Use raw in salads.
Collards	*Brassica oleracea* Acephala Group	Leaves/shoots	Cook lightly like cabbage leaves.
		Flowering heads	Use like broccoli.
		Flowers	Use raw in salads.
Columbine	*Aquilegia vulgaris*	Leaves (note: seeds and roots are toxic and should not be eaten)	See page 69.
		Flowers	Use raw sprinkled on salads.
Cornelian cherry	*Cornus mas*	Fruits	Harvest full ripe or else allow to after-ripen to remove astringency. Then very nice eaten raw, makes good jams and fruit leathers and can be used in cooked desserts after removing seeds.

Plant		Part	Cooking tips / page references
Crab apples	*Malus* spp.	Fruits	Sometimes sweet enough to eat raw, otherwise use like cooking apples.
Cranberries	*Vaccinium macrocarpon* & *V. oxycoccos*	Fruits	Normally eaten cooked and sweetened in dessert dishes, or the juice is mixed with other sweeter juices. See page 33 (drying).
Creeping dogwood	*Cornus canadensis*	Fruits	Mediocre flavour, best used cooked with other fruits or in mixed jams.
Daffodil garlic	*Allium neapolitanum*	Leaves/shoots	Lovely mild garlic flavour, excellent raw in salads and sandwiches, also used cooked lightly.
		Flowers	Use in salads.
Damson	*Prunus insititia*	Fruits	Normally cooked, skins are slightly bitter. Good in cooked desserts, jams, etc.
Dandelion	*Taraxacum officinale*	Leaves	See page 71.
		Flowers	See page 71.
		Roots	Traditionally roasted, ground and used like coffee.
Date plum	*Diospyros lotus*	Fruits	Harvest after leaves fall and fruits colour, or allow to after-ripen, so that astringency has gone. Nice raw or the pulp can be used in desserts.
Day lilies	*Hemerocallis* spp.	Flowers	See page 118.
		Shoots	Use in spring in moderation – mild onion flavour; put them in salads or cook lightly.
		Roots	Cook like other root crops - boil, roast, etc. They are of finger thickness with a nutty, salsify flavour.
Devon sorb apple	*Sorbus devoniensis*	Fruits	Eat fresh, or use pulp in desserts or fruit leather mixes.
Earthnut pea	*Lathyrus tuberosus*	Tubers	These are starchy and are used in all the same ways as small potatoes – boil, roast, fry, etc. The flavour is similar to that of sweet potatoes.
Egyptian onion	*Allium cepa* Proliferum Group	Leaves/shoots	See page 202.
		Bulbs	These have a mild onion flavour and used in all the same ways as true onion.
Elephant garlic	*Allium ampeloprasum* var. *ampeloprasum*	Leaves	Young leaves can be eaten in salads and cooked. They have a leek-garlic flavour.
		Bulbs	See page 121.
European elder	*Sambucus nigra*	Flowers	Many traditional uses including elderflower cordial, wine and 'champagne'; also battered and fried.
		Fruits	Best cooked with other fruits or made into wine.
False strawberry	*Duchesnea indica*	Fruits	Flavourless, but juicy and seeds on outside are crunchy – can add interest to a salad.
		Young leaves	Mild flavour, best used in salads.
Fennel	*Foeniculum vulgare*	Leaves/stems	See page 73.
		Seeds	Widely used in cooking and herb teas.
Fig	*Ficus carica*	Fruits	Mostly eaten fresh. See page 33 (drying).

Plant		Part	Cooking tips / page references
Flowering quince (japonica)	*Chaenomeles japonica*	Fruits (note: seeds are poisonous and should not be eaten)	See page 161.
French scorzonera	*Reichardia picroides*	Leaves/shoots	These have a lovely mild cucumber flavour and tender texture through the growing season – use in salads.
French sorrel	*Rumex scutatus*	Leaves/shoots	Same as other sorrels. See page 139.
Fuchsias	*Fuchsia* spp.	Fruits	Best eaten raw, with a peppery-plum flavour.
Gages	*Prunus domestica*	Fruits	These are the sweetest and most delicious plum-type fruits and should be eaten fresh.
Garlic chives	*Allium tuberosum*	Leaves	The flat leaves have a mild garlic flavour, good raw in salads, in sandwiches, and cooked lightly in any dish needing garlic flavouring.
Garlic cress	*Peltaria alliacea*	Leaves	Used raw in salads or cooked – strong garlic/mustard flavour.
Garlic mustard (also known as Jack-by-the-hedge)	*Alliaria petiolata*	Leaves/shoots	Use in salads or in cooked dishes (particularly later in the season when fiery hot raw).
		Seeds	Use whole, or grind and use like mustard seeds.
Giant butterbur (also known as fuki / sweet coltsfoot)	*Petasites japonicus*	Leaf stalks	See page 75.
Globe artichoke	*Cynara cardunculus* Scolymus Group	Flower buds	One of the few well-known perennial vegetables.
Goji berry	*Lycium barbarum*	Fruits	Best to shake ripe fruit off bushes over a sheet – handled fruit can deteriorate quickly. Slightly bitter raw; much better eaten after drying.
		Leaves/shoots	Leaves and very young shoots are cooked lightly as a vegetable, and then resemble a slightly mint-flavoured spinach.
Golden garlic	*Allium moly*	Leaves/shoots	Use like garlic chives.
		Flowers	Bright yellow, use in salads.
Good King Henry	*Chenopodium bonus-henricus*	Leaves/shoots	See page 77.
Gooseberry	*Ribes uva-crispa*	Fruits	Use fresh or cooked.
Goumi	*Elaeagnus multiflora*	Fruits	Wait until fully ripe for astringency to disappear, then use fresh or, like autumn olive, in jams and fruit leathers.
Grapes	*Vitis* spp.	Fruits	Use fresh and for wine; see page 33 (drying).
		Leaves	Use young leaves to wrap food prior to cooking.
Groundcover raspberries	*Rubus* 'Betty Ashburner', *R. nepalensis* & *R. tricolor*	Fruits	Like raspberries, best eaten raw as they do not have a long shelf life after harvesting. Also use in jams.
Groundnut	*Apios americana*	Tubers	See page 204.
Hawthorns	*Crataegus* spp.	Young leaves	Use raw in salads and sandwiches. See page 163.
		Fruits	See page 163 and page 38 (fruit leather).

Plant		Part	Cooking tips / page references
Hazels	*Corylus* spp.	Nuts	See page 167 and page 40 (drying).
Heartnut	*Juglans ailantifolia* var. *cordiformis*	Nuts	Use in all the same ways as walnut.
		Sap	Tapped in late winter, can be drunk fresh (slightly sweet), otherwise best made into wine.
Hedge mustard	*Sisymbrium officinale*	Leaves/shoots	Use in salads or in cooked dishes (particularly later in the season when fiery hot raw).
		Seeds	Use whole or ground like mustard seed.
Herb patience	*Rumex patientia*	Leaves	Use cooked just as for sorrel leaves.
Hickories	*Carya laciniosa* & *C. ovata*	Nuts	Use like pecan nuts; excellent raw or in cooked dishes. The nuts require a heavy-duty nutcracker.
Hog peanut	*Amphicarpaea bracteata*	Buried seeds	Like peanut, this plant buries some of its seedpods into the ground. These seeds are bean-flavoured and can be eaten raw or cooked like other beans.
Holm oak	*Quercus ilex*	Nuts (acorns)	See oaks. Holm oak seeds are lower in tannin content than most other oaks.
Honesty	*Lunaria annua*	Leaves/shoots	Mustard-flavoured, tender; used in salads.
		Flowers	Also used in salads.
		Roots	Taproots are like miniature mouli radishes with the same flavour, and are used in the same ways.
Hop	*Humulus lupulus*	Shoots	See page 79.
Horseradish	*Armoracia rusticana*	Young leaves	These are tender and peppery in spring, great in salads.
		Roots	The well-known sauce is made of these. Extremely hot!
Hostas	*Hosta* spp.	Shoots	See page 82.
Ice plant	*Sedum spectabile*	Leaves/shoots	See page 85.
Japanese pepper (also known as sansho)	*Zanthoxylum piperitum*	Fruits	The pinky-red fruit 'shell' is peppery and aromatic (the seed is tasteless); grind in a peppermill or by pestle and mortar and use instead of black pepper.
Japanese plum	*Prunus salicina*	Fruits	Use in the same way as plums, fresh or in fruit leathers, etc.
Japanese wineberry	*Rubus phoenicolasius*	Fruits	See page 172.
Jerusalem artichoke	*Helianthus tuberosus*	Tubers	Well-known perennial vegetable, used cooked.
Jostaberry	*Ribes* x *culverwellii*	Fruits	Mainly eaten fresh. Much sweeter than blackcurrants and could make a nice leather.
Judas tree	*Cercis siliquastrum*	Flowers	Use in salads in spring.
Juneberries	*Amelanchier* spp.	Fruits	Eaten fresh, cooked with other fruits or in mixed fruit leathers.
		Flowerheads	Use like broccoli. You must prevent it from flowering so you'll want to harvest these!
Kiwis	*Actinidia* spp.	Fruits	Mainly eaten fresh or used in desserts. See page 33 (drying).
Korean mint	*Agastache rugosa*	Leaves/shoots	These are used as a minty-anise flavouring in salads and cooked dishes.
Land cress	*Barbarea verna*	Leaves/shoots	Peppery flavour, used raw in salads, sandwiches, etc.

Plant		Part	Cooking tips / page references
Lemonade bush	*Rhus aromatica*	Fruit heads	Harvest when fruit turns red. The whole head of berries can be soaked overnight in water to make a lemon-flavoured drink. Individual fruits can also be stripped and agitated in water to extract more flavour.
Lemon balm	*Melissa officinalis*	Leaves/shoots	Use fresh for herb teas and in salads.
Lesser stitchwort	*Stellaria graminea*	Leaves/shoots	See page 87.
Limes	*Tilia* spp.	Young leaves	See page 125.
Lingonberry	*Vaccinium vitis-idaea*	Fruits	These are acid and somewhat bitter (like cranberries) – usually made into jam or other preserves.
Liquorice	*Glycyrrhiza glabra*	Roots	Harvest roots in autumn/winter, chop into sections and dry to store. Boil dried roots to make herb teas; they can also be chewed fresh or dried.
Loganberry	*Rubus x loganobaccus*	Fruits	Use fresh or cooked.
Lovage	*Levisticum officinale*	Leaves/shoots	Use through spring and early summer for flavouring. Has a yeasty-celery flavour, excellent especially in soups and stews.
		Seeds	Dry seed is harvested late summer and stores well. Grind in a pestle and mortar to use the same flavouring in winter stews and soups.
Maidenhair tree	*Ginkgo biloba*	Nuts	Cook by boiling for 5-10 minutes or roasting; eat by itself or put cooked nuts into savoury dishes.
Mallows	*Malva* spp.	Leaves	See page 127.
		Flowers	Very pretty in salads.
Maples/sycamore	*Acer* spp.	Sap	Tapped in late winter, can be drunk fresh (slightly sweet), otherwise best made into wine.
Marsh mallow	*Althaea officinalis*	Leaves	Best eaten cooked as a spinach-type vegetable, or used to thicken soups and stews.
		Roots	Cook by any method; best mixed with other ingredients as their flavour is very mild.
Mashua	*Tropaeolum tuberosum*	Tubers	See page 207.
		Leaves	These are peppery like other nasturtiums; great added to salads.
		Flowers	Also good and very colourful in salads.
Maypop	*Passiflora incarnata*	Fruit pulp	Fruits ripen in autumn and contain some pulp with seeds, similar to true passionfruit; used in exactly the same ways, usually raw in desserts.
Medlar	*Mespilus germanica*	Fruits	See page 176 and page 38 (fruit leather).
Mints	*Mentha* spp.	Leaves/shoots	Best used raw in salads or for herb teas. Fine in cooked dishes too, but add near the end so the flavour isn't lost.
Mirabelle	*Prunus cerasifera*	Fruits	The best-flavoured varieties should be eaten fresh. Some varieties are sweet but more mediocre in flavour, and are useful for making early season fruit leathers.
Mitsuba (also known as Japanese parsley)	*Cryptotaenia japonica*	Leaves/shoots	Use raw in salads and for seasoning (especially with fish). Flavour has elements of angelica, parsley and celery.

Plant		Part	Cooking tips / page references
Monkey puzzle	*Araucaria araucana*	Nuts	These are starchy and are eaten cooked, e.g. boiled for 5 minutes or roasted. They have a lovely chestnut / tropical plantain flavour. If boiled they can then be added to stews, etc.
Mountain pepper	*Drimys lanceolata*	Seeds	Harvest seeds in autumn and dry to store. Grind in a pepper mill and use as a direct substitute for black pepper.
		Young leaves	Tender young leaves are also peppery and good in salads.
Mountain sorrel	*Oxyria digyna*	Leaves	See page 129.
Mulberries	*Morus* spp.	Fruits	Eat fresh or use raw in desserts.
		Leaves	Leaves of white and red mulberries and their hybrids are an excellent cooked spinach-type vegetable. Use the leaves instead of spinach, e.g. layered in pies, lasagnes, etc. High in protein.
Multiplier onions	*Allium cepa* Aggregatum Group	Leaves	Use raw in salads or lightly cooked.
		Bulbs	Use like shallots or small onions.
Myrtle	*Myrtus communis*	Leaves/shoots	Use for flavouring, raw or dried. Mainly used in soups or in marinades for its spicy citrus flavour.
Nanking cherry	*Prunus tomentosa*	Fruits	Eat fresh.
Nectarine	*Prunus persica*	Fruits	Mainly eaten fresh. See page 33 (drying).
Nepalese pepper	*Zanthoxylum armatum*	Fruits	The pinky-red fruit 'shell' is peppery and aromatic (the seed is tasteless); grind in a peppermill or by pestle and mortar and use instead of black pepper.
Nepalese raspberry (also known as groundcover raspberry)	*Rubus nepalensis*	Fruits	Like raspberries, best eaten raw as they do not have a long shelf life after harvesting. Also in jams.
New Jersey tea	*Ceanothus americanus*	Leaves	Leaves are harvested in summer before flowering, and dried. Used to make herb tea with a similar flavour and aroma to 'standard' tea (*Camellia sinensis*).
New Zealand flax	*Phormium tenax*	Nectar	Flowers are very high in nectar. One of the few flowers it really is worth sucking the nectar from!
		Seeds	These are aromatic and best used in bread, cakes, biscuits, etc.
Oaks	*Quercus* spp.	Nuts (acorns)	See page 179.
Oca	*Oxalis tuberosa*	Tubers	See page 209.
		Leaves/shoots	The foliage looks very similar to wood sorrel and has a similar lemony acid flavour. Good used in moderation in salads.
Oleaster	*Elaeagnus angustifolia*	Fruits	Harvest when fully ripe, when astringency will disappear.
Oregano	*Origanum vulgare*	Leaves/shoots	Use fresh for flavouring many dishes including meats, also raw in salads. Leaves dry well.
Oregon grapes	*Mahonia* spp.	Fruits	Harvested in summer; fruits are quite acid but make good jams and preserves.
Orpine	*Sedum telephium*	Leaves/shoots	See page 89.

Plant		Part	Cooking tips / page references
Ostrich fern	*Matteuccia struthiopteris*	Young shoots	See page 91.
Oyster mushroom	*Pleurotus ostreatus*	Mushrooms	Great is savoury cooked dishes of all kinds, or simply fried as a side dish.
Partridge berry	*Mitchella repens*	Fruits	Little flavour so best with other fruits in desserts, jams or fruit leathers.
Pawpaw	*Asimina triloba*	Fruits	The large fruits, which ripen in autumn, are eaten fresh or the pulp is scooped out and used in desserts. The flesh is creamy, custard-like and the flavour a mixture of mango, pineapple and banana.
Peach	*Prunus persica*	Fruits	Mainly eaten fresh. See page 34 (drying).
Pear (European)	*Pyrus communis*	Fruits	Mainly eaten fresh. Cooking varieties are boiled or roasted. See page 34 (drying) and page 38 (fruit leather). Perry pear fruits are harvested from the ground and the juice fermented in the same way as for apples, to make the drink perry.
Pecan	*Carya illinoinensis*	Nuts	Eaten fresh and in desserts.
Peppermint	*Mentha x piperita*	Leaves/shoots	Mainly used for herb teas. There are many good-flavoured varieties of peppermint including Black peppermint and Swiss mint. The leaves dry well.
Perennial broccoli	*Brassica oleracea* Botrytis Group	Leaves/shoots	Use steamed like cabbage.
		Flowerheads	Similar to small cauliflower heads, and used in all the same ways.
Perennial kale	*Brassica oleracea* Ramosa Group	Leaves/shoots	Use in the same ways as ordinary kale.
Persimmons	*Diospyros kaki, D. lotus & D. virginiana*	Fruits	Mainly eaten fresh once any astringency has disappeared. See page 34 (drying).
Pig nut	*Bunium bulbocastanum*	Tubers	These are starchy and eaten cooked – roasted or boiled – and have a lovely chestnut flavour.
		Leaves/shoots	The foliage resembles parsley in flavour and is used raw in salads.
Pines	*Pinus* spp.	Seeds	Pine nuts are used in pesto, raw in salads and also cooked in many Mediterranean dishes.
Plantains	*Plantago* spp.	Leaves/shoots	See page 132.
Plum	*Prunus domestica*	Fruits	Used raw and cooked, also made into jam and very useful as a sweetener in fruit leathers. See page 34 (drying).
Plum yews	*Cephalotaxus* spp.	Fruits	Eat raw or use the pulp for flavouring desserts with a butterscotch / pine nut flavour.
		Seeds	The shelled seeds resemble peanuts in flavour and are usually eaten as a snack food in the same way.
Poke root (also known as pokeweed / poke)	*Phytolacca americana*	Young shoots	Harvest young shoots in late spring. Cook by placing in cold water, bring to the boil, then change the water for fresh boiling water. Boil for 10-15 minutes. The shoots then have an earthy asparagus flavour – serve with butter, a sauce or mayonnaise. (Note: raw shoots are toxic and should not be eaten.)

Plant		Part	Cooking tips / page references
Pot marigold	*Calendula officinalis*	Leaves	These are tender with a very nice aromatic flavour and are good added to salads.
		Flowers	Tear the petals off the flowerhead and scatter into salads – very colourful.
Quamash	*Camassia quamash*	Bulbs	Harvest late winter. Long, slow cooking makes the bulbs much more digestible – for example, use a slow cooker for 12 hours or more. Once cooked, the flavour and texture is similar to sweet potato.
Quince	*Cydonia oblonga*	Fruits	See page 185.
Rampion	*Campanula rapunculus*	Roots	Long taproots, like thin parsnips, are harvested in winter and cooked by boiling or roasting. The cooked flavour is sweet and walnut-like.
Ramps	*Allium tricoccum*	Leaves	Use in all the same ways as ramsons.
Ramsons (also known as wild garlic)	*Allium ursinum*	Leaves	See page 95.
Raspberry	*Rubus idaeus*	Fruits	Mainly eaten fresh and in desserts. See page 38 (fruit leather).
		Leaves	Harvested in summer and dried, then used to make herb teas.
Redcurrant	*Ribes rubrum*	Fruits	Used fresh, in desserts and for jam.
Red valerian	*Centranthus ruber*	Leaves/shoots	Harvest through the growing season. The leaves are tender with a flavour resembling broad beans. Use fresh in salads.
Redwood sorrel	*Oxalis oregana*	Leaves/shoots	Use like other sorrels, in moderation, and fresh in salads, etc.
Rhubarbs	*Rheum* spp.	Leaf stalks	See page 97 and page 34 (drying).
Roses	*Rosa* spp.	Flowers	All good in salads.
		Fruits	Rosehips of all species can be used similarly to apple rose, but most are smaller and therefore more fiddly to prepare.
Rosebay willowherb (also known as fireweed)	*Epilobium angustifolium*	Leaves/shoots	The young leaves and shoots have a flavour resembling asparagus and can be used in salads or as a cooked vegetable or ingredient.
Rosemary	*Rosmarinus officinalis*	Leaves/shoots	The well-known herb.
Rowan	*Sorbus aucuparia*	Fruits	Rowan fruits are bitter and traditionally used for make a jelly served with meat.
Sage	*Salvia officinalis*	Leaves/shoots	The well-known herb.
		Flowers	These have a lovely mild sage flavour and are great sprinkled in salads.
Salad burnet	*Sanguisorba minor*	Leaves/shoots	Mild-flavoured, suitable for using in decent quantities in salads.
Saltbushes	*Atriplex canescens* & *A. halimus*	Leaves/shoots	These have a slightly salty flavour and can be used fresh in salads or cooked lightly as a vegetable, or added late into stir-fries.

Plant		Part	Cooking tips / page references
Saskatoon	*Amelanchier alnifolia*	Fruits	Mainly eaten fresh, but also make good jams and fruit leathers.
Sea beet	*Beta vulgaris* subsp. *maritima*	Leaves/shoots	See page 135.
Sea buckthorn	*Hippophae rhamnoides*	Fruits	The orange fruits are very juicy and acid. The juice from them can be mixed with sweeter fruit juices or sweetened another way and drunk. The fruits make an excellent jam and can also be included in mixed fruit leathers.
Sea kale	*Crambe maritima*	Young leaves	Cook like cabbage leaves.
		Flowerheads	These look and taste just like broccoli and can be used in all the same ways.
		Flowers	The flowers have a honey-like flavour and are used in salads or desserts.
		Roots	These are starchy, so are cooked by boiling or roasting. Best cooked together with other vegetables, as the flavour is very mild.
Service tree	*Sorbus domestica*	Fruits	Harvest when fully ripe, when any astringency should have disappeared. Nice to eat fresh or you can use just like apples. If astringent they are best used for cider.
Salal (also known as shallon)	*Gaultheria shallon*	Fruits	Often eaten fresh. See page 19 (traditional preserves).
Sheep's sorrel	*Rumex acetosella*	Leaves/shoots	Use like other sorrels. See page 139.
Shiitake mushroom	*Lentinula edodes*	Mushrooms	See page 212.
Siberian pea tree	*Caragana arborescens*	Young pods	Harvest before they start to get tough. Eat fresh or cooked like mangetout peas – they taste similar.
		Seeds	These also taste like fresh peas. You can harvest them young and eat raw or later when they will need cooking. Dried seed should be soaked overnight then cooked.
Siberian purslane	*Claytonia sibirica*	Leaves/shoots	See page 215.
Silverweed	*Potentilla anserina*	Roots	These are starchy and are cooked, e.g. by boiling or roasting (roots are long and narrow so do not take long to cook). Nice stir-fried with other vegetables, as the flavour is very mild.
Skirret	*Sium sisarum*	Roots	See page 218.
Snowbell tree (also known as silverbell tree)	*Halesia carolina*	Young fruits	See page 137.
Solomon's seals	*Polygonatum* spp.	Young shoots	See page 100.
Sorrels	*Rumex* spp.	Leaves/shoots	See page 139.
Spearmint	*Mentha spicata*	Leaves/shoots	Another mint that makes very nice herb teas. Harvest leaves to dry just before flowering; they dry well.
Spinach beet (also known as perpetual spinach) & chard	*Beta vulgaris* subsp. *cicla*	Leaves/shoots	Use in just the same ways as spinach, e.g. in stir-fries, pies, lasagnes or on its own.
Stinging nettle	*Urtica dioica*	Leaves/shoots	See page 103.

Plant		Part	Cooking tips / page references
Strawberries	*Fragaria* spp.	Fruits	Mainly eaten fresh and in desserts. See page 34 (drying).
		Young leaves	Young leaves of all strawberry species are tender and mild-flavoured, good for adding into salads.
Strawberry tree	*Arbutus unedo*	Fruits	Harvest when the fruits redden in late autumn (before they are ripe they have stone cells like pears and are inedible). They have a sweet, delicate flavour and are eaten fresh, and made into wine and liqueur.
Sugar maple	*Acer saccharum*	Sap	Tapped in late winter, can be drunk fresh (slightly sweet), otherwise best made into wine.
Sumachs	*Rhus glabra* & *R. typhina*	Fruit heads	Harvest when fruits turn red. The whole head can be soaked overnight in water to make a lemon-flavoured drink. Individual fruits can also be stripped and agitated in water to extract more flavour.
Sweet cicely	*Myrrhis odorata*	Leaves/shoots	See page 188.
		Young seeds	See page 188.
		Roots	The taproots look like parsnips but also have a lovely anise flavour. They are eaten fresh or cooked just like other root crops.
Sweet peas (annual and perennial)	*Lathyrus odoratus, L. latifolius* & *L. sylvestris*	Seeds	Eat fresh but in moderation (they can be toxic in excess); most species have seeds with a nice pea flavour.
Sweet tea vine	*Gynostemma pentaphyllum*	Leaves/shoots	Harvest these fresh or dry them, and use for herb teas. Widely used in China where it is regarded as an adaptogen like ginseng, which strengthens the immune system.
Szechuan pepper	*Zanthoxylum schinifolium* & *Z. simulans*	Fruits	See page 190.
		Leaves	Young leaves can be used as a flavouring in cooked dishes and added to pickles and chutneys.
Tibetan whitebeam	*Sorbus thibetica*	Fruits	Eaten raw, cooked or preserved like medlars.
Trifoliate orange	*Poncirus trifoliata*	Fruits	Harvest in autumn. The skin can be used in marmalades, and the juice pressed from fruits then used like lemon juice.
Turkish rocket	*Bunius orientalis*	Leaves/shoots	See page 142.
		Flowerheads	See page 142.
		Flowers	See page 142.
Ulluco	*Ullucus tuberosus*	Tubers	These have a nutty flavour and crisp texture and can be eaten raw – for example sliced in salads – or cooked like potatoes.
Violets	*Viola* spp.	Flowers	These are used in salads.
		Leaves	Also used in salads, but can also be used in cooked dishes when they have a thickening effect.
Walnut	*Juglans regia*	Nuts	See page 193 and page 40 (drying).
		Sap	Tapped in late winter, can be drunk fresh (slightly sweet), otherwise best made into wine.
Watercress	*Nasturtium officinale*	Leaves/shoots	Well known, used fresh in salads, sandwiches, etc. Also used cooked, and makes fantastic soup.

Plant		Part	Cooking tips / page references
Wax myrtle (also known as bayberry)	*Myrica cerifera*	Leaves	Similar in flavour to true bay, and can be used in all the same ways, but does not dry so well.
Welsh onion	*Allium fistulosum*	Leaves	See page 145.
		Bulbs	These can be used just like shallots or small onions.
Whitebeam	*Sorbus aria*	Fruits	Fruits of all the whitebeams are mealy (as opposed to juicy), with a flavour between medlar and almond. When fully ripe, they are all nice to eat fresh, and the pulp is also good in mixed fruit leather and desserts.
Whitecurrant	*Ribes rubrum*	Fruits	Used fresh, in desserts and for jam. It is the same species as redcurrant.
Wild angelica (also known as wood angelica)	*Angelica sylvestris*	Leaves/shoots	These can be used in the same ways as the more common biennial angelica – fresh as a flavouring, in cooked dishes, or, traditionally, candied.
Winter purslane (also known as miner's lettuce)	*Claytonia perfoliata*	Leaves/shoots	Related to Siberian purslane, and with a similar beetroot-type flavour. Can be used raw in salads or added into stews, soups, etc. for just a few minutes of cooking.
Wood sorrel	*Oxalis acetosella*	Leaves/shoots	Best used raw in salads, to give a lemony tang.
Worcesterberry	*Ribes divaricatum*	Fruits	These are like small sweet gooseberries and can be used in all the same ways; very nice raw.
Yacon	*Smallianthus sonchifolia*	Tubers	See page 221.
Yams (also known as air potatoes)	*Dioscorea* spp.	Tubers	See page 224.
		Air tubers	See page 224.
Yellow asphodel (also known as king's spear)	*Asphodeline lutea*	Shoots	Treat like asparagus; just cook lightly for a few minutes and serve as a vegetable with butter, sauce or mayonnaise.
Yellowhorn	*Xanthoceras sorbifolium*	Seeds	Shelled seeds have a very nice Brazil nut flavour and are excellent when eaten fresh. They can also be used cooked, or dried and ground into a flour like chestnuts. The flour is then used in breads, pancakes, etc.

Appendix 2: Plants by month of use

This table shows when the plants featured in Part 2 of this book are available to use fresh during the year in UK conditions. So, although a plant may be listed in the 'spring' section, for example, you may find it is also available at other times of the year.

Plant			Jan	Feb	Mar	Apr	May	Jun	Jul	Aug	Sep	Oct	Nov	Dec
Alexanders (black lovage)	*Smyrnium olusatrum*	Leaves/shoots		●	●	●	●							
		Seeds						●						
		Roots	●	●	●								●	●
American elder	*Sambucus canadensis*	Flowers							●	●	●	●	●	
		Fruits								●	●			
Apple mint	*Mentha suaveolens*				●	●	●	●	●	●	●	●	●	
Apple rose (rugosa rose)	*Rosa rugosa*	Flowers					●	●	●	●				
		Fruits									●	●		
Autumn olive	*Elaeagnus umbellata*										●	●		
Babington's leek (perennial leek)	*Allium ampeloprasum* var. *babingtonii*	Bulbils								●				
		Stems/leaves	●	●	●	●	●					●	●	●
Bamboos	*Phyllostachys* spp., *Pleioblastus simonii*, *Pseudosasa japonica*, *Semiarundinaria fastuosa* and *Yushania* spp.					●	●	●	●					
Beech	*Fagus sylvatica*						●							
Cardoon	*Cynara cardunculus*	Flower buds							●	●	●			
		Leaf stalks				●	●	●	●	●	●	●		
Chestnuts	*Castanea* spp.										●	●	●	
Chicory	*Cichorium intybus*	Leaves/shoots					●	●	●	●	●	●		
		Roots	●	●	●	●						●	●	●
Chinese artichoke	*Stachys affinis*		●	●	●							●	●	●
Chinese cedar (toon)	*Toona sinensis*						●	●						

Plant			Jan	Feb	Mar	Apr	May	Jun	Jul	Aug	Sep	Oct	Nov	Dec
Columbine	*Aquilegia vulgaris*	Leaves				•	•	•	•	•	•			
		Flowers				•	•	•						
Dandelion	*Taraxacum officinale*	Leaves	•	•	•	•	•							
		Flowers				•	•	•						
		Roots	•	•	•							•	•	•
Day lilies	*Hemerocallis* spp.	Flowers						•	•	•	•			
		Shoots				•	•	•	•	•	•	•		
		Roots	•	•	•	•						•	•	•
Egyptian onion	*Allium cepa* Proliferum Group		•	•	•	•	•	•	•	•	•	•	•	•
Elephant garlic	*Allium ampeloprasum* var.*apeloprasum*	Leaves	•	•	•	•	•							
		Bulbs										•	•	•
Fennel	*Foeniculum vulgare*						•	•	•	•	•	•		
Flowering quince (japonica)	*Chaenomeles japonica*									•	•	•	•	
Giant butterbur (fuki / sweet coltsfoot)	*Petasites japonicus*					•	•							
Good King Henry	*Chenopodium bonus-henricus*						•	•	•	•	•	•		
Groundnut	*Apios americana*		•	•								•	•	•
Hawthorns	*Crataegus* spp.	Young leaves				•	•							
		Fruits									•	•		
Hazels	*Corylus* spp.										•	•		
Hop	*Humulus lupulus*					•	•	•						
Hostas	*Hosta* spp.					•	•							
Ice plant	*Sedum spectabile*					•	•	•	•	•	•			
Japanese wineberry	*Rubus phoenicolasius*									•	•			
Lesser stitchwort	*Stellaria graminea*					•	•	•	•					
Limes	*Tilia* spp.						•	•	•	•	•	•		
Mallows	*Malva* spp.	Leaves	•	•	•	•	•	•	•	•	•	•	•	•
		Flowers					•	•	•					

Appendix 2: Plants by month of use

Plant			Jan	Feb	Mar	Apr	May	Jun	Jul	Aug	Sep	Oct	Nov	Dec
Mashua	*Tropaeolum tuberosum*	Tubers	●	●	●							●	●	●
		Leaves				●	●	●	●	●	●	●		
		Flowers										●	●	
Medlar	*Mespilus germanica*											●	●	
Mountain sorrel	*Oxyria digyna*				●	●	●	●	●	●	●	●		
Oaks	*Quercus* spp.											●	●	
Oca	*Oxalis tuberosa*	Tubers										●	●	●
		Leaves/shoots					●	●	●	●	●	●		
Orpine	*Sedum telephium*						●	●	●	●	●	●		
Ostrich fern	*Matteuccia struthiopteris*					●	●							
Plantains	*Plantago* spp.					●	●	●	●	●				
Quince	*Cydonia oblonga*											●	●	
Ramsons (wild garlic)	*Allium ursinum*			●	●	●	●	●						
Rhubarbs	*Rheum* spp.			●	●	●	●	●						
Sea beet	*Beta vulgaris* subsp. *maritima*						●	●	●	●	●	●		
Shiitake mushroom	*Lentinula edodes*						●	●	●	●	●	●	●	●
Siberian purslane	*Claytonia sibirica*		●	●	●	●	●	●	●	●	●	●	●	●
Skirret	*Sium sisarum*		●	●	●							●	●	●
Snowbell tree (silverbell tree)	*Halesia carolina*								●					
Solomon's seals	*Polygonatum* spp.						●	●						
Sorrels	*Rumex* spp.					●	●	●	●	●	●	●		
Stinging nettle	*Urtica dioica*				●	●	●							
Sweet cicely	*Myrrhis odorata*	Leaves/shoots				●	●	●	●	●	●	●		
		Young seeds						●	●	●	●	●		
		Roots	●	●	●								●	●
Szechuan pepper	*Zanthoxylum schinifolium* & *Z. simulans*	Fruits										●	●	
		Leaves					●							

Plant			Jan	Feb	Mar	Apr	May	Jun	Jul	Aug	Sep	Oct	Nov	Dec
Turkish rocket	*Bunias orientalis*	Leaves/shoots				●	●	●	●	●	●	●		
		Flower-heads & flowers						●	●	●				
Walnut	*Juglans regia*	Nuts										●		
		Sap			●	●								
Welsh onion	*Allium fistulosum*	Leaves				●	●	●	●	●	●	●		
		Bulbs	●	●	●							●	●	●
Yacon	*Smallianthus sonchifolia*											●	●	●
Yams (air potatoes)	*Dioscorea* spp.	Tubers	●	●	●	●							●	●
		Air tubers										●	●	

Resources

Further information

Agroforestry Research Trust
www.agroforestry.co.uk
Charitable organisation, of which Martin Crawford is Director. Researches and teaches about unusual species and agroforestry systems, and sells seeds and plants of edible and useful species.

http://permacultureplate.blogspot.co.uk
Caroline Aitken's blog. Information about permaculture, forest gardening and cooking, including seasonal recipes and a journal from Caroline's smallholding.

www.patrickwhitefield.co.uk
Information about permaculture, including the courses taught by Patrick Whitefield and Caroline.

Equipment

The supplier lists given here are not exhaustive, but provide an indication of the types of company selling useful equipment.

Apple and Nut Wizards
www.applewizard.com, (01624) 829394 (for UK enquiries)
www.nutwizard.com, (+1) 812 275 1016 (US supplier)

Apple corer, slicer & peeler
www.harrodhorticultural.com, 0845 402 5300
www.creamsupplies.co.uk, 0845 226 3024
www.divertimenti.co.uk, 0870 129 5026
www.suntekstore.co.uk
www.wayfair.co.uk, 0800 169 0423
www.juiceland.co.uk, 0845 009 0309

Dehydrators
www.ukjuicers.com, 01904 757070
www.juiceland.co.uk, 0845 009 0309
www.energiseyourlife.com, 020 7794 8485
www.detoxyourworld.com, 08700 113 119
www.wholisticresearch.com, 01763 284910

Fermentation crocks
purenature24.co.uk, 0800 121 7330

Grain mills
www.hawos.de, +49 (0) 6172 401200
www.hehlis-holistics.co.uk, 020 8660 7954

Hand-operated nut cracker
www.handcranknutcracker.com, (+1) 530 273 9378 (USA)

Harvesting comb (berry picker)
www.raymears.com, 01580 819668
www.harrodhorticultural.com, 0845 402 5300

Plug-in timer switches
These are available from any electrical store.

Solar driers (self-build advice)
www.builditsolar.com
http://practicalaction.org/solar-drying-4

Telescopic fruit picker
www.worldofwolf.co.uk, 020 8829 8850
www.abbeygardensales.co.uk, 01822 614053 / 0845 124 9410

Vacuum packing machines
www.juiceland.co.uk, 0845 009 0309

Books

The Forager Handbook (2009), Miles Irving. Ebury Press

Hugh's Three Good Things (2012), Hugh Fearnley-Whittingstall. Bloomsbury Publishing

A Taste of the Unexpected (2010), Mark Diacono. Quadrille Publishing

The Thrifty Forager (2011), Alys Fowler. Kyle Books

Wild Fermentation (2003) and *The Art of Fermentation* (2012), Sandor Ellix Katz. Chelsea Green Publishing

Picture credits

Page 85: http://commons.wikimedia.org/wiki/File:Sedum_spectabilum_a1.jpg by Selso

Page 95: http://commons.wikimedia.org/wiki/File:Stara_Planina-03.JPG by Infobgv

Page 107: iStockphoto

Page 118: http://commons.wikimedia.org/wiki/File:Hemerocallis_middendorffii_02.jpg by Algirdas

Page 179: http://commons.wikimedia.org/wiki/File:Quercus_robur_Marki.JPG by Crusier

Pages 183 and 184: Toni Spencer, The Feral Kitchen

Page 185: http://commons.wikimedia.org/wiki/File:Quitte_Cydonia_oblonga-2.jpg by Dkrieger

Index of recipes

The majority of the recipes in this book are vegetarian. Those that are not are indicated here with an asterisk (*).

Index

Also by Green Books

"This is a seminal piece of work on truly sustainable gardening, written with great spirit and soul" – Alys Fowler

Forest gardening is a novel way of growing crops, with nature doing most of the work for you. As well as familiar plants you can grow edibles such as goji berries, yams, heartnuts and bamboo shoots. This 'bible' on the subject covers design, planting and maintenance, for plots large and small, and includes a detailed directory of over 500 trees, shrubs, herbaceous perennials, root crops and climbers. *384 pages, hardback*

"This lovely book makes it clear that we are not just missing a trick, we are missing a feast"
– Hugh Fearnley-Whittingstall

Perennial vegetables are a joy to grow and require a lot less time and effort than annuals. They also extend the harvesting season, especially in early spring, and are often higher in mineral nutrients. This book provides comprehensive advice on all types of perennial vegetable (edibles that live longer than three years), from ground-covers and coppiced trees to bog and woodland plants. It features over 100 species in detail, and includes plenty of cooking tips. *224 pages*

"A really well organised, approachable yet thorough guide"
– Mark Diacono

This clear, practical guide, for both amateur and expert, explains all you need to know in order to grow delicious fruit – from planting your trees to harvesting your produce. It covers all the common tree fruits and some more unusual ones, with recommended varieties of each. It advises on how to deal with all the pest and disease problems you may encounter, while the mysteries of pruning are illuminated with step-by-step instructions and detailed diagrams. *352 pages*

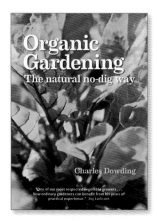

"One of our most respected vegetable growers" – Joy Larkcom

Charles Dowding has been growing organic vegetables commercially for 30 years, without digging the soil. In this new, full-colour edition of *Organic Gardening* he shares the wealth of his experience, explaining his approach to soil and plants and revealing the techniques that enable him to grow wonderfully healthy and vibrant crops. He describes how to grow a wide range of fruit and vegetables: what varieties to choose, when to sow and how to avoid pests and diseases. *240 pages*

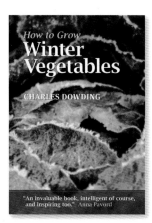

"A comprehensive, practical and inspiring guide" – Sarah Raven

This beautiful book shows how to enjoy an abundance of vegetables at the darkest time of year, as well as through the 'hungry gap' of early spring. Although not much grows in winter, a well-organised plot can be quite full. You need to plan carefully – as early as spring – for sowing and planting at the right times throughout the year. The main part of the book is a month-by-month sowing, planting and growing calendar. Other sections cover harvesting and storing your produce, and growing salad leaves through winter. *232 pages*

About Green Books

Join our mailing list:
Find out about forthcoming titles, new editions, special offers, reviews, author appearances, events, interviews, podcasts, etc.
www.greenbooks.co.uk/subscribe

How to order:
Get details of stockists and online bookstores, or order direct from our website. Bookstores: find out about our distributors or contact us to discuss your particular requirements.
www.greenbooks.co.uk/order

Send us a book proposal:
If you want to write, we'd love to hear from you. We aim to make the process of book-writing as satisfying and as easy as possible.
www.greenbooks.co.uk/for-authors